1-2-3 Magic for Christian Parents

Effective Discipline for Children 2-12

1-2-3 Magic

for

Christian Parents

Thomas W. Phelan, Ph.D.
Chris Webb, M.S., M.A.

ParentMagic, Inc.
Glen Ellyn, Illinois

All scripture quotations, unless otherwise indicated, are taken from the HOLY BIBLE, NEW INTERNATIONAL VERSION® (NIV). Copyright © 1973, 1978, 1984 by International Bible Society. All rights reserved.

Other Scripture quotations are taken from the following sources:

The New King James Version® (NKJV). Copyright © 1982 by Thomas Nelson, Inc. All rights reserved. The Message: The New Testament in Contemporary English by Eugene Peterson. Copyright © 1993, 1994, 1995, 1996, 2000. All rights reserved. Holy Bible NEW LIVING TRANSLATION (NLT), Copyright © 1996 by Tyndale House Publishers. All rights reserved. The New American Standard Bible (NASB), Copyright © 1960, 1962, 1963, 1968, 1971, 1972, 1973, 1975, 1977, 1995 by The Lockman Foundation. All rights reserved.

Illustrations by Dan Farrell
Distributed by Independent Publishers Group

Printed in the United States of America
10 9 8 7 6 5 4 3 2 1

For more information, contact: ParentMagic, Inc.
800 Roosevelt Road
Glen Ellyn, Illinois 60137

Publisher's Cataloging-in-Publication

(Provided by Quality Books, Inc.)

Phelan, Thomas W., 1943-
  1-2-3 magic for Christian parents / Thomas W. Phelan, Chris Webb.
    p. cm.
    Includes index.
    ISBN-13: 978-1-889140-24-7
    ISBN 1-88914-024-4

    1. Discipline of children--Religious aspects--Christianity. 2. Child rearing--Religious aspects--Christianity. I. Webb, Chris, 1967- II. Title.
    III. Title: One two three magic for Christian parents.
    IV. Title: 123 magic for Christian parents. V. Title: Christian parents.

HQ770.4.P45 2007   649'.6408827
                          QBI07-600202

To our children who were raised with 1-2-3 Magic:

Reagan, Kennedy, John Walker,
Julie and Tom

Thanks for bringing joy to our lives.

Contents

PART III: NO CHILD WILL THANK YOU

PART IV: ENCOURAGING GOOD BEHAVIOR

PART V: STRENGTHENING YOUR RELATIONSHIP

Preface

Behold, children are a heritage from the Lord, the fruit of the womb is a reward.

Psalm 127:3 (NKJV)

My wife and I were truly excited as God blessed us with one, then two, and finally three children. We totally agreed with the psalmist that children were indeed a gift from God.

However, when all three were under the age of six, we also identified with the writer of Proverbs when he wrote "Foolishness is bound up in the heart of a child." Our desire was to raise our children in a Christian home and pass on our faith and values. In reality, we were frustrated and struggled just to get through the day and hope the kids stayed in bed most of the night. I felt guilty from getting angry so often and felt inadequate to teach my children about the things of God.

On top of all that, I was an ordained minister and supposed to be an example for others to follow. As I was praying and searching during this difficult time, I stumbled across a parenting book by Dr. Thomas Phelan entitled *1-2-3 Magic: Effective Discipline for Children 2-12*. This book proved to be an answer to my prayer. I immediately began to see how Dr. Phelan's simple principles of parenting connected with scripture. His ideas included practical ways to implement biblical concepts.

My wife and I decided to give it a try. The results were amazing.

i

Not only were we able to manage our family better, we also were more in control of our emotions. We spent less time trying to discipline our kids and more time enjoying them and nurturing their spiritual life.

I've since taught many parents this program through individual Christian counseling and through church conferences. The response has been overwhelming. The reason for the success of *1-2-3 Magic: Effective Discipline for Children 2-12* is simple. The program is easy to learn and it works. You can learn it one day and start it the next. There really is no "magic" involved, but many delighted parents believe that the 1-2-3 works like magic.

I've teamed up with Dr. Phelan to offer a Christian edition of this incredible parenting plan. Our goal in *1-2-3 Magic for Christian Parents* is to provide practical materials that will make a dramatic and positive difference in the lives of the people who use this program. We want Christian parents around the country to enjoy their children and to be able to discipline them with gentleness, firmness and decisiveness. This will be a valuable aid in assisting children to grow up happy, competent and able to get along with others.

How to Use This Book

1-2-3 Magic for Christian Parents describes some straightforward and very effective methods for managing the behavior of children from the ages of approximately two to twelve. You do not have to be a genius, saint or professional psychotherapist to use this program well. To get the best results, keep in mind the following:

1. The methods should be used exactly as they are described here, especially with regard to the No-Talking and No-Emotion Rules.

2. If both parents are living at home, both adults should use the techniques. If one parent refuses to use *1-2-3 Magic*, however, the other parent can still use it on his or her own (while hoping, of course, that their spouse is doing something reasonable with the kids).

3. Single parents can use our methods effectively by themselves. In fact, single parents will greatly benefit from a simple and effective system like the 1-2-3, since these adults are overloaded, don't have a lot of time

to spend learning discipline programs, and cannot afford to be inefficient when it comes to managing their children.

4. Grandparents, babysitters and other caregivers have also found the 1-2-3 very helpful in managing young children. Actually, in the past, many grandparents first discovered *1-2-3 Magic* on their own and then shared it with their children. We also hear more and more these days that many grandparents are raising their grandchildren themselves, and these adults often find the *1-2-3 Magic* program to be a lifesaver.

5. Make sure your kids are in good physical health. It is a well-known fact that illness, allergies and physical pain can both aggravate as well as cause behavioral and emotional problems in children. Regular physical exams for the kids are of critical importance.

6. Chapters 1-11 *must* be read before starting with counting and before using the methods in chapters 12-26 as well. Some parents, in fact, use counting for seven to ten days to get the house under control, then they proceed with Part IV, Encouraging Good Behavior.

Psychological Evaluation and Christian Counseling

Psychological evaluation and Christian counseling are indicated *before* using *1-2-3 Magic for Christian Parents* if any child has a history of excessive separation anxiety, physical violence or extremely self-punitive behavior. These children can be exceptionally difficult to manage during the initial testing period when they are still adjusting to the new discipline. If a family is currently in counseling, this program should be discussed with the counselor before being used. If your counselor is not familiar with *1-2-3 Magic for Christian Parents*, bring a copy of the book for him or her to become familiar with.

Psychological evaluation and counseling are indicated *after* using *1-2-3 Magic for Christian Parents* if:

1. Marital instability or conflict are interfering with the effective use of the methods. *1-2-3 Magic* is normally an excellent way to get mom and dad "on the same page" in dealing with the kids. Sometimes just a few counseling sessions can help right the ship.

2. One or both parents are incapable of following the No-Talking and No-Emotion Rules. Other life stresses, as well as problems such as anxiety and depression, can make it hard for some parents to calm down enough to effectively use *1-2-3 Magic for Christian Parents*. Talking this difficulty over with a therapist can help get mom or dad back on track.

3. Behavior problems, as well as testing and manipulation by the child, are continuing at too high a level for more than three weeks after starting the program. Say your child was hard to manage before using 1-2-3. Now he's better, but you still feel managing him is too much of a grind. Check this out with a mental health professional.

4. Trust your instincts. Here's a good rule of thumb: If you have been worrying about a particular problem in your child for more than six months, that's too long. See someone and find out if there is, in fact, something wrong. If there is, try to fix it or learn how to manage it. If there's nothing wrong, stop worrying.

Serious psychological and behavioral problems in young children frequently include persistent difficulties with the following:

- Paying attention or sitting still
- Language development, social interaction, and restricted interests
- Negative, hostile and defiant behavior
- Excessive worrying or unusual anxiety about separation
- Loss of interest in fun activities and irritability
- Excessive verbal and physical aggression
- Disregard for age-appropriate norms and rules
- Unexpected learning difficulties

Parenting: Not for the Faint of Heart!

*Discipline your children; you'll be glad you did—
they'll turn out delightful to live with.*

Proverbs 29:17 The Message

"Can I have a Twinkie?"

"No, dear."

"Why not?"

"'Cause we're eating at six o'clock."

"Yeah, but I want one."

"I just told you you couldn't have one."

"You never give me anything!"

"What do you mean I never give you anything? Do you have clothes on? Is there a roof over your head? Am I feeding you in two seconds?!"

"You gave Joey one a half-hour ago."

"Listen, are you your brother? Besides, *he* eats his dinner."

"I promise I'll eat my dinner."

"Don't give me this promise, promise, promise stuff, Monica! Yesterday—at 4:30—you had half a peanut butter and jelly sandwich and you didn't eat anything at dinner!"

"THEN I'M GOING TO KILL MYSELF AND THEN RUN AWAY FROM HOME!!"

1

Good Discipline, Good Times

The only people who think parenting and teaching are easy are those who have never done either one. The Bible places a high priority on these jobs, but they can be some of the most difficult assignments. Living with young children can be one of life's most enjoyable experiences, yet it can become unbelievably frustrating. This frustration can be reduced if you're better equipped to deal with the difficulties kids present.

Adults with romantic notions of parenting often forget that it is impossible to give kids everything they want. Raising and educating children means that, in addition to nurturing and supporting them, you must frustrate them on a regular basis—for their own good and for the good of everyone. Children deserve grace but they also need justice.

Consider what the Bible teaches: "Discipline your children while you still have the chance; indulging them destroys them" (Proverbs 19:18 The Message). "Now it's time for bed. Now you must do your homework. Stop teasing your sister. No, you can't have the Twinkie." Over and over, firmness and gentleness are required.

Unfortunately, when they are frustrated, kids do not usually thank their parents for trying to raise them properly. Even the writer of Hebrews noted this, "No discipline seems pleasant at the time, but painful. Later on, however, it produces a harvest of righteousness and peace for those who have been trained by it" (Hebrews 12:11).

Youngsters have an amazing, natural ability to confuse, sidetrack and aggravate adults. We call this "testing and manipulation," and there are six basic types (Chapter 10). Testing and manipulation can eliminate fun, destroy affection, impair learning and—over the long run—ruin relationships.

Repeat the Twinkie scene above a thousand times and you have guaranteed misery. That's no way for anyone to live and certainly no way for any child to grow up.

The Bible gives many great principles for raising children. The difficulty comes in application. That is where *1-2-3 Magic for Christian Parents* can help. This program is a great way to "Discipline your children..." (Proverbs 19:18a) in a fair, perfectly clear and non-abusive way. *1-2-3 Magic for Christian Parents* helps adults know how to handle difficult behavior, encourage good behavior and manage the inevitable sidetrack of testing and manipulation.

When children's troublesome behavior is handled in routine and successful ways, the warmer side of parenting is allowed to kick in. Affection, talking and listening, praise and shared fun can flow naturally. Good discipline, in other words, makes for good times and good relationships. Said another way: "Discipline your children; you'll be glad you did— they'll turn out delightful to live with" (Proverbs 29:17 The Message).

1-2-3: Three Steps to Effective Parenting

1-2-3 Magic for Christian Parents will provide you with three steps for effective parenting. Each of the three steps is distinct, manageable and extremely important. The three parenting steps are also mutually interdependent; in other words, each one depends to some extent on the others for its success. Ignore any of these steps at your own risk.

Parenting Step 1 (Parts II and III) involves controlling obnnoxious behavior. You will never like or get along well with your children if they are constantly irritating you with their whining, arguing, teasing, badgering, tantrums, yelling and fighting. In *1-2-3 Magic for Christian Parents* you will learn how to "count" obnoxious behavior, and you will be pleasantly surprised at how effective that simple technique is!

Step 2 (Part IV) involves encouraging good behavior. Encouraging good behavior, such as picking up after yourself, going to bed (and staying in bed), being courteous, getting up and out in the morning, and doing homework, takes more effort—for both parent and child—than controlling difficult behavior. You will learn seven simple methods for encouraging positive actions in your kids.

Finally, in Step 3 (Part V) you will learn some valuable and not-so-difficult ways of maintaining healthy relationships with your children. Some parents merely need to be reminded of these strategies; other parents have to work hard at them. Paying attention to the quality of your relationship with your children will help you with Steps 1 and 2. And success with Steps 1 and 2, in turn, will allow you to enjoy your youngsters and want to spend time with them.

Important Note for Christian Parents

As a Christian parent, there are several things you should keep in mind as we begin. First, your personal relationship with Jesus will provide you the most benefit in parenting. Please take time daily to connect with Him. Second, the simple 1-2-3 program will help you get control of your household so you can spiritually nurture you children's faith. You can't be a good spiritual leader if all your time and energy is spent on trying to control your kids. Finally, get ready to experience God in new ways as you explore biblical principles of parenting and the practical applications of these principles with *1-2-3 Magic for Christian Parents*.

Let's get going—and good luck!

Points to Remember...

The 3 Steps to Effective Parenting

1. Controlling obnoxious behavior
2. Encouraging good behavior
3. Strengthening your relationship with your child

Part I

Straight Thinking

1

Is It Magic?

Train up a child in the way he should go, and when he is old he will not turn from it.

Proverbs 22:6

1-2-3 Magic for Christian Parents is not magic. Instead, it is a simple, precise and effective way of managing—gently and firmly—the behavior of children in approximately the two-to-twelve-year-old age range. The reason for our unusual title is that so many parents, teachers and other child caretakers have said, "It works like magic!" *1-2-3 Magic for Christian Parents* certainly does work if you do it correctly, which means following a few basic rules. The 1-2-3 is what you might call a "parents-in-charge" strategy. The plan is a way to help your children follow the biblical admonition to "...obey your parents in the Lord, for this is right." (Ephesians 6:1). And best of all, no arguing or yelling will be necessary.

The 1-2-3 program is currently being used all over the world by millions of parents, teachers, grandparents, day care workers, babysitters, summer camp counselors, hospital staff and other child caretakers. This plan has been translated into many foreign languages, including Korean, Italian, Spanish, Japanese and Chinese. The 1-2-3 is also being taught and recommended by thousands of ministers, mental health professionals and pediatricians.

7

The method described in this book is easy to master. You can start the program right away. You do not have to be a saint, genius or professional psychotherapist to use the 1-2-3 properly. Too many parenting programs start by pointing out the fifty to seventy-five mistakes you are supposedly making with your kids at the present time. Then, in the hope of helping you to correct these errors, the program presents fifty to seventy-five elaborate parenting strategies that require an advanced degree in psychology in order to be able to use them properly. The result? You are left with bad feelings, confusion, and no clear place to start. Worse than that, things in your house stay the same.

Quik Tip...

After reading the *1-2-3 Magic for Christian Parents* book, start the program right away. Just thinking about it will not change your kids' behavior one bit. But be ready—things are going to change quickly!

After reading *1-2-3 Magic for Christian Parents*, however, you will know exactly how to apply the key biblical principles of discipline using the 1-2-3 plan. You will know exactly what to do, what not to do, what to say and what not to say in just about every one of the common, everyday problem situations you run into with your kids. Because *1-2-3 Magic for Christian Parents* is based on only a few basic, but critical concepts, you will be able not only to remember what to do, you will be able to do it when you are anxious, agitated or otherwise upset (which for many of us parents is every day!). You will also be able to be a kind but effective parent when you are busy, in a hurry or otherwise preoccupied.

In addition to managing minor but frequent parenting problems, you will also know how to handle more serious difficulties, such as lying, stealing and fighting. With *1-2-3 Magic for Christian Parents* there is—surprisingly—much less in the way of technique and strategy to remember. That fact is extremely important when an adult is trying to deal with an emotionally charged situation involving a child. Paul writes in the New Testament, "...do not exasperate your children; instead bring them up in the training and instruction of the Lord" (Ephesians 6:4).

1-2-3 Magic for Christian Parents can help you avoid exasperating your children even in the midst of difficult circumstances. The strategies of this book are straightforward and the parenting guesswork is minimal.

You will find that if you use the 1-2-3 correctly, it will work! The 1-2-3 has been shown to be very effective with two-to-twelve-year-olds, whether they are "problem" children or just typical youngsters. In fact, *1-2-3 Magic for Christian Parents* has been used successfully with learning disabled, attention deficit and emotionally disturbed children as well as with visually impaired and hearing impaired kids. It has been used with developmentally and mentally impaired kids. To benefit properly from the 1-2-3, the only rule is that a child must have a mental age of about two.

The book of James says, "...be you doers of the word and not hearers only, deceiving yourselves" (James 1:22 NKJ). When you read and understand the scriptural principles and the discipline plan in *1-2-3 Magic for Christian Parents*, it is a good idea to start immediately. Talk with your spouse and get going right away. If you are a single parent, take a deep breath and then explain the drill to your youngsters. Do the same thing if you're a grandparent. If you don't start right away, you may never get around to it.

If you are a minister, Christian counselor, or pediatrician, suggest that your church members, clients, or patients get a copy of the book *1-2-3 Magic for Christian Parents* at their local bookstore, or consider providing them with one.

What to Expect When You Begin the 1-2-3

When you do start *1-2-3 Magic for Christian Parents*, things will change quickly. But there is good news and bad news. The good news is that initially about half of all kids fall into the "immediate cooperator" category. They seem to intuitively understand when the Bible says, "Take good counsel and accept correction—that's the way to live wisely and well" (Proverbs 19:20 The Message). What do you do? Just relax and enjoy your good fortune!

The bad news is that the other half of the kids will fall into the "immediate tester" category. These children will get worse first. They will challenge you to see if you really mean business with your new parenting ideas. If you stick to your guns, however—not arguing, yelling or hitting—you will get the vast majority of these little testers shaped up pretty well in about a week to ten days. Then what do you do? You start enjoying your children again.

Believe it or not, you may soon have a much more peaceful home and more enjoyable kids. You will go back to liking and respecting yourself as a parent—all in the foreseeable future! You will be able to echo the sentiments of the psalmist when he said, "Like arrows in the hand of a warrior, so are the children of one's youth. Happy is the man who has his quiver full of them" (Psalm 127:4-5 NKJV).

Before we get into the details of the 1-2-3, we must clarify two very important concepts:

1. The two basic types of problem behavior (Chapter 2).
2. The dangerous assumption parents and other caretakers make about young children (Chapter 3).

Points to Remember...

Once you start using *1-2-3 Magic for Christian Parents*, there's good news and bad news. Children will fall into one of two categories:

1. Immediate cooperators
2. Immediate testers

Enjoy the cooperators and brace yourself for the testers!

Questions for Christian Practice

1. Read Proverbs 13:18, 29:15, 29:17 and 19:16. What do these verses have to say about the importance of discipline?

2. Describe your current discipline plan or plans. Rate the effectiveness of them on a scale from 1-10.

3. Describe times when it is more difficult to deal with your children's minor but irritating behaviors.

4. Describe a recent situation where your child exhibited irritating behavior. How did you respond?

5. If your discipline attempts were videotaped for a week for a reality show, would it be more like Jerry Springer or Leave It To Beaver? Explain your answer.

2
Stop Behavior and Start Behavior

Remind the people to be subject to rulers and authorities, to be obedient, to be ready to do whatever is good.

Titus 3:1

Paul tells us in the book of Titus to remind people to be obedient and to do good. As Christian parents it's our job to implement these principles with our children. When you are frustrated with your youngsters, the kids are either (1) doing something you want them to *Stop*, or (2) they are not doing something you would like them to *Start*. In *1-2-3 Magic for Christian Parents* we call these two kinds of things "Stop" behavior and "Start" behavior.

In the hustle and bustle of everyday existence, you may not have worried much about the difference between Start and Stop behaviors, but—as we'll soon see—the distinction is extremely important. This distinction is also about to make your life a lot easier! Stop behavior includes the frequent, minor, everyday hassles kids present to you, such as whining, disrespect, tantrums, arguing, teasing, fighting, pouting, yelling and so on. Stop behavior—in and of itself—ranges from mildly irritating to obnoxious. Each of these difficult behaviors alone may not be so bad, but add them all up in one afternoon and by 5 p.m. you may feel like hitchhiking to South America.

Start behavior includes positive activities like cleaning rooms, doing homework, practicing the piano, getting up and out in the morning, going to bed, eating supper and being nice to other people. You have a Start behavior problem when your child is not doing something that, in your eyes, would be a good thing to do.

With Stop behavior problems, therefore, the issue is what the kids *are doing*. With Start behavior problems, the issue is what the kids *are not doing*. The reason for distinguishing between these two kinds of behaviors is this: You will use different tactics for each kind of problem.

Quik Tip...

With Stop behavior, the issue is what the kids **are doing**. With Start behavior, the issue is what the kids **are not doing**. There are different tactics for each kind of problem. Don't worry, you'll soon be an expert in no time!

For Stop behavior, such as whining, arguing, screaming and teasing, you will use the 1-2-3, or "counting" procedure. Counting is simple, gentle and direct.

For Start behavior problems, you will have a choice of seven tactics, which can be used either singly or in combination. These tactics include Praise, Simple Requests, Kitchen Timers, The Docking System, Natural Consequences, Charting and a Variation of the 1-2-3. Start behavior strategies, as you can probably guess, require a little more thought and effort than counting does.

Why the difference in strategies? The answer lies in the issue of motivation. How long does it take a child—if she is motivated—to terminate a Stop behavior like whining, arguing or teasing? The answer is about one second; it's really not a big project. And—depending on how angry or oppositional a child is—terminating an obnoxious behavior doesn't take tons of effort.

But now look at Start behavior. How long does it take a child to eat dinner? Maybe twenty to twenty-five minutes. To pick up after himself? Perhaps fifteen minutes. To get ready for bed? Twenty to thirty minutes. Ready for school? Thirty minutes. How about homework? Schoolwork might take anywhere from forty minutes to three years. So it's obvious that with Start behavior, more motivation is required from the child. He has to begin the project, keep at it and then finish it. And the project is often something the boy or girl is not thrilled about having to do in the first place.

In addition, if encouraging positive behavior in kids requires more motivation in the kids, it's also going to require more motivation from mom and dad. As you'll soon see, putting an end to Stop behavior using counting is relatively easy if you do it right. Start behavior is harder.

When managing a behavioral difficulty with one of your children, therefore, you will need to first determine if you have a Stop or a Start behavior problem. Is the issue something I want the child to quit? Or is it something I want the youngster to get going on? Since counting is so easy, one of the biggest problems we run into is parents using counting for Start behavior; for example, counting a child to get her to do her homework. As you will soon see, counting produces motivation that usually lasts only a short time (from a few seconds to a couple of minutes) in children. If you mix up your tactics (e.g., use counting for homework), you will not get optimum results.

But don't worry. This whole procedure is so simple, you'll be an expert in no time. Effective discipline will start to come naturally and—believe it or not—your kids will start listening to you. But first, you must learn to think realistically—and not wishfully—about your kids. You may have a dangerous false assumption floating around in your head about young children.

Points to Remember...

For **Stop behavior**, such as:

Whining
Teasing
Arguing
Pouting
Yelling
Tantrums

Use the 1-2-3, or "counting" procedure.

For **Start behavior**, such as:

Picking up
Eating
Homework
Bedtime
Up and out

Use Praise, Simple Requests, Kitchen Timers, The Docking System, Natural Consequences, Charting or the 1-2-3 Variation.

Questions for Christian Practice

1. Read Proverbs 15:5, 1:8-9, Exodus 20:12 and Ephesians 6:1-3. Why is it important for children to obey their parents?

2. Describe the difference between "Stop" and "Start" behavior.

3. Describe a time when you struggled to "Stop" (whining, teasing, pouting, etc) a behavior in your child? Describe a time when you struggled trying to get your child to "Start" (Picking up, eating, homework, etc) a behavior.

4. List the "Stop" behaviors you would like to address with your child.

5. List the "Start" behaviors you would like to see happen with your child.

3

The Little Adult Assumption

*When I was a child, I talked like a child, I thought like a child,
I reasoned like a child.*

I Corinthians 13:11

M any parents and teachers carry around in their heads a trouble-
producing notion about young children. This idea is a kind of false
assumption or wish that causes discipline attempts that don't work, along
with stormy scenes that make everyone feel bad. This erroneous concept
is known as the "Little Adult Assumption."

The Little Adult Assumption is the belief that kids have hearts of
gold and that they are basically reasonable and unselfish. They're just
smaller versions of grownups, in other words. And because they are little
adults, this notion goes, whenever the youngsters are misbehaving or not
cooperating, the problem must be that they don't have enough information
at their disposal to be able to do the right thing.

Imagine, for example, that your eight-year-old son is torturing his
little sister for the fifteenth time since they got home from school. What
should you do? If your boy is a little adult, you simply sit him down,
calmly look him in the eye, and explain to him the three golden reasons
why he shouldn't tease his sister. First of all, teasing hurts her. Second, it
makes you mad at him. Third—and most important—how would he feel
if someone treated him like that?

Your son looks at you, his face brightening with insight, and he says, "Gee, I never looked at it like that before!" Then he stops bothering his sister for the rest of his life. That would certainly be nice, but any veteran parent or teacher knows that scenes like that don't happen. Kids are not little adults.

The crucial point here is this: Grownups who believe—or want to believe—the Little Adult Assumption are going to rely heavily on words and reason in dealing with young kids and trying to change their behavior. And words and reasons by themselves, are going to be miserable failures much of the time. The Bible says, "A servant cannot be corrected by mere words; though he understands, he will not respond" (Proverbs 29:19). What is true of servants in this context applies equally to children. It will take more than explanations for kids to change. Furthermore, explanations can take the parent and child through what we call the Talk-Persuade-Argue-Yell-Hit Syndrome.

What is that? Imagine your child is doing something you don't like. You read in a parenting book that you should talk the problem out no matter how long it takes. So you try telling your daughter why she shouldn't be doing what she's doing. She doesn't respond, so you next try to persuade her to see things your way. When persuasion fails, you start arguing with the little girl. Arguing leads to a yelling match, and when that fails, you may feel there is nothing left to do but hit. Actually, ninety-nine percent of the time that parents scream, hit and spank their children, the parent is simply having a temper tantrum. The tantrum is a sign that (1) the parent doesn't know what to do, (2) the parent is so frustrated that he or she can't see straight, and (3) this adult has an anger management problem.

We're not implying that you are going around hitting your kids all the time. It may be true, however, that the chief cause of child abuse (physical abuse, not sexual) is the Little Adult Assumption. A parent reads in a book that talking and reasoning is the preferred method. When talking and reasoning fail, however, the parent goes crazy and starts hitting, because his favorite strategy isn't working and desperation has set in.

As we'll clarify more later, talking and explaining certainly have their place in raising children. The writer of Ecclesiastes said there is, "...a time to speak..." (Ecclesiastes 3:7). But kids are just kids—not little adults. Years ago one writer said, "Childhood is a period of transitory psychosis."

She meant that kids, when they are little, are—in a way—sort of nuts! They are not born reasonable and unselfish, they are born unreasonable and selfish. Consequently, it is the parent's job—and the teacher's job—to help kids become the opposite. In accomplishing this goal, adults need to be gentle, consistent, decisive and calm.

How do you do that? You start by changing your thinking about children and by getting rid of the Little Adult Assumption. In order to get this erroneous notion out of parents' heads, we use a bit of what we call "cognitive shock." Although it's a little exaggerated and may sound strange, think of it like this: Instead of imagining your kids as little adults, think of yourself as a *wild animal trainer*! We don't mean, of course, using whips, guns or chairs. And we certainly don't mean being nasty.

But what does a wild animal trainer do? He chooses a method—which is largely nonverbal—and repeats it until the "trainee" does what he, the trainer, wants. The trainer is patient and gentle, but also persistent. Our job in *1-2-3 Magic* is to present some useful training methods to you, so that you can repeat them until the trainees, your children, do what you want them to. Fortunately, you do not usually have to repeat these methods for very long before you get results. And you can gradually add more talking and reasoning as the kids get older. But remember this: One explanation—if necessary—is fine. It's the attempts at repeated explanations that get adults and children in trouble.

> **CAUTION**
>
> One explanation, if really necessary, is fine. It's the attempts at *repeated explanations* that get adults and kids into trouble. Too much parent talking irritates and distracts children.

Dictatorship to Democracy

The overall orientation of *1-2-3 Magic* is what you might call "dictatorship to democracy." When your kids are little, your house should be pretty much a benign dictatorship where you are the judge and jury. Your two-year-old, for example, cannot decide to go out and play in the street, no matter how much he wants to. And your four-year-old cannot arbitrarily opt—at 7:30 in the morning on Wednesday—to skip preschool because she wants to stay home and play with the new toy she just got for her birthday.

When the kids are in their mid-to-late teens, though, your house should be more of a democracy. The youngsters should have more to say about the rules and policies that affect them. You should be having family meetings from time to time to iron out differences (Chapter 19). Even when the kids are teens, though, when push comes to shove, who's paying the mortgage? You are. And who knows better than the kids do what's good for them? You do. And, when necessary, you have a right—and a duty—to impose limits on your children, even if they don't like it.

Too many parents these days are afraid of their children. What are they afraid of? Physical attack? Not usually. What many parents fear is that their children won't like them. So, in a conflict situation, these parents explain and explain and explain, hoping the child will eventually come around. All too often, these parental efforts simply lead to the Talk-Persuade-Argue-Yell or Talk-Persuade-Argue-Yell-Hit Syndrome.

What if you have children who always respond to words and reasons? You are certainly lucky! Recent research has indicated that there are three such children in this country. If you have one or more of them, you may not need this book. Or, if your kids ever stop responding to logic, you can consider using the 1-2-3.

So what is this training method we're talking about? We first have to explain what it is not.

Key Concepts...

Noncompliance and lack of cooperation in children are not always due to lack of information. Kids are not little adults or simply small computers, so raising youngsters involves training as well as explaining.

Questions for Christian Practice

1. Read Titus 2:4, Deuteronomy 11: 18-19, 1 Timothy 3:4. What are the parents' responsibilities concerning their children?

2. Describe a time when you were guilty of the Little Adult Assumption.

3. Describe a time when you got angry with your child? How did words and reasoning play a part?

4. Do you think the "Wild Animal Trainer" is a good analogy for parenting? Why or why not?

5. Describe an occasion when you were a benevolent dictator with your child. Describe a time when you practiced democracy.

4

The Two Biggest
Discipline Mistakes

A fool gives full vent to his anger, but a wise man keeps himself under control.

Proverbs 29:11

When words are many, sin is not absent. but he who holds his tongue is wise.

Proverbs 10:19

The two biggest mistakes that parents make in dealing with children are these: Too Much Talking and Too Much Emotion. The Bible clearly teaches that "... he who holds his tongue is wise" (Proverbs 10:19b). This is especially true dealing with children because constant talking not only doesn't work, but it can also take you through the Talk-Persuade-Argue-Yell-Hit-Syndrome. Ironically, too much talking and explaining makes kids less likely to cooperate because it irritates and distracts them.

The Bible also teaches we should be self-controlled. The wise writer of Proverbs wrote, "Better a patient man than a warrior, a man who controls his temper than one who takes a city" (Proverbs 16:32). We should show our excitement and emotion when we are expressing affection towards our children, not when we are upset with their behavior. Again, Proverbs tells us why. "An angry man stirs up dissension and a hot-tempered one commits many sins" (Proverbs 29:22).

Angry adults can yell, scream, belittle and nag; they can also physically endanger their kids. *1-2-3 Magic for Christian Parents* is as much a way for parents to practice self-control as it is a way to manage children's behavior.

There is another reason why too much emotion can interfere with effective parenting and effective teaching. When they are little, kids feel inferior. They feel inferior because they *are* inferior. They are smaller, less privileged, less intelligent, less skillful, less responsible and less of just about everything than their parents and the older kids. And this "lessness" bugs them a lot. They don't like it. They do like to feel they are powerful and capable of making some mark on the world.

Key Concepts...

If you have a child who is doing something you don't like, get real upset about it on a regular basis and, sure enough, she'll repeat it for you!

Watch your two-year-olds. They want to be like the five-year-olds, who can do a lot more neat things. The five-year-olds, in turn, want to be like the ten-year olds. And the ten-year-olds want to be like you; they want to drive cars and use cell phones and credit cards! They want to have some impact on the world and to make things happen.

Have you ever seen a small child go down to a lake and throw rocks in the water? Children can do that for hours, partly because the big splashes are a sign of their impact. They are the ones causing all the commotion.

What does throwing rocks in the water have to do with what happens at home? Simple. If your little child can get big-old-you all upset, *your upset is the big splash for him.* Your upset makes your child feel powerful. His reacting this way does not mean that he has no conscience and is going to grow up to be a professional criminal. It's just a normal childhood feeling: Having all that power temporarily rewards—or feels good to—the inferior part of the child. Parents who say, "It drives me absolutely crazy when she eats her dinner with her fingers!! Why does she do that?!" may have already answered their own question. She may do that—at least partly—*because it drives them crazy.*

An important rule, therefore, is this: If you have a child who is doing something you don't like, get real upset about it on a regular basis and, sure enough, she'll repeat it for you.

When it comes to discipline, you want to be consistent, decisive and calm. So what we recommend in *1-2-3 Magic for Christian Parents* is that you apply—during moments involving conflict or discipline—what we call the "No-Talking and No-Emotion" rules. Since we're all human, these two rules really mean very little talking and very little emotion. *This point is absolutely critical to your effectiveness.* There are discipline systems other than the 1-2-3, but you will ruin any of them by talking too much and getting too excited. These two mistakes, of course, usually go hand in hand, and the emotion involved is usually anger.

Some parents and teachers can turn off the talking and the emotional upset like a faucet, especially once they see how effective it is to keep quiet at the right time. Other adults, however, have to bite their lips bloody to get the job done. I saw a T-shirt the other day that said, "Help me — I'm talking and I can't stop!" For some people, it seems, talking comes almost too naturally.

If you have trouble with talking too much, how do you accomplish the difficult goal of remaining calm and quiet in a discipline situation? Lots of moms, dads and teachers simply tell themselves over and over and over again that talking, arguing, yelling and screaming not only don't help, they actually make things worse. They continually remind themselves that these "tactics" merely blow off steam for a few seconds.

Other parents have found it useful to memorize and recite Bible verses to themselves. Proverbs 29:11 and 10:19 found at the beginning of this chapter are good verses to use for this purpose. It can also be very helpful to pray for strength when tempted to talk. The very act of praying itself will serve to interrupt the useless chatter.

If, after a month to six weeks of using *1-2-3 Magic*, parents find that they can't shake these habits, it's time to face facts: Some sort of outpatient evaluation and counseling is indicated (for the adult, not the child!).

Points to Remember...

No Talking!
No Emotion!

Questions for Christian Practice

1. Read James 1:19, 3:1-12, Ecclesiastes 7:9. What does the Bible have to say about our words and anger?

2. How well do you practice the spiritual fruit of "self-control" and "patience" when dealing with the annoying behavior of your child? Explain.

3. Describe a time when you relied too heavily on words when dealing with a discipline situation. What were the results?

4. Describe a time when you got emotional or upset with your child.

5. How will you remind yourself not to talk or get upset when you are disciplining your child?

Part II

Controlling Obnoxious Behavior

5

Counting Obnoxious Behavior

Foolishness is bound up in the heart of a child.
Proverbs 22:15a (NKJV)

You want your children to learn to think and take responsibility for their own behavior. The Bible calls this self-control. Nagging, complaining, and getting angry usually do not motivate children to greater self-control. Change and growth occur when someone faces consequences. Consider God's view: "A man reaps what he sows. The one who sows to please his sinful nature, from that nature will reap destruction; the one who sows to please the Spirit, from the Spirit will reap eternal life" (Galatians 6:7-8). Children need to experience consequences from their actions in order to change. The challenge for parents is this: Just how do you implement the consequences children need to help them gain self-control?

One of the first giant parenting steps involves controlling obnoxious behavior. Let's face it; children can be obnoxious. The writer of Proverbs understood this when he wrote, "Foolishness is bound up in the heart of a child..." (Proverbs 22:15a NKJV)). We'll describe the 1-2-3 or counting method to help parents deal with this foolishness and help their children gain self-control. Counting is surprisingly powerful and deceptively simple, but you have to know what you're doing.

First, remember that you will use the 1-2-3, or counting method, to deal with Stop (obnoxious or difficult) behavior. You will be counting things like arguing, fighting, whining, yelling and tantrums. You will not use the 1-2-3 to get the child up in the morning, to get her to do her homework or to motivate her to practice the piano.

Second, if you are new to *1-2-3 Magic*, you will be skeptical. The procedure will seem too easy or perhaps not tough enough. Some of you will think, "Hey, you don't know my kid. This kid is a wild man!"

Don't worry about feeling skeptical. The 1-2-3 *is* deceptively simple, but it is not always easy. The "magic" is not in the counting. Anyone can count. The magic—or what may seem like magic—is in the No-Talking and No-Emotion rules, which make children think and take responsibility for their own behavior.

Of course, there really is no magic in *1-2-3 Magic for Christian Parents*. It just seems that way. The program is a way of implementing certain biblical principles and it is also backed up by behaviorial research. Soon—when conflicts with kids arise—you will feel like a new person: consistent, decisive and calm.

Undoubtedly, after our initial explanation, you will have questions. We will attempt to answer all of your questions in the next chapter. After that, and after you have read through the information in chapters 6-10, you can begin counting.

Counting Difficult Behavior

How does the 1-2-3 work? Imagine you have a four-year-old child (some of you don't have to imagine!). This child is having a major temper tantrum on the kitchen floor at 6 p.m. because you—in your hardness of heart—would not give him a small bag of potato chips right before dinner. Your son is banging his head on the floor, kicking your new kitchen cabinets, and screaming bloody murder. You are sure the neighbors can hear the noise all the way down the block, and you're at a loss for what to do.

Your pediatrician told you to ignore your son's tantrums, but you don't think you can stand it. Your mother told you to put a cold washcloth on the kid's face, but you think her advice is strange. And your husband told you to spank the boy.

None of these is an acceptable alternative. Instead, with the 1-2-3, you hold up one finger, look down at your noisy little devil, and calmly say, "That's 1."

He doesn't care. He's insane with rage and keeps his tantrum going full blast. You let five seconds go by, then you hold up two fingers and say, "That's 2." You get the same lousy reaction; the tantrum continues. So after five more seconds, you hold up three fingers and say, "That's 3, take 5."

Now what does all this mean? It means that your son was just given two chances—the first two counts—to shape up. But in this instance he blew it—he didn't shape up. So there is going to be a consequence. The consequence can be a "rest period" or "time out" (about one minute per year of the child's life), or the consequence can be what we call a "time out alternative" (loss of a privilege or toy for a period of time, bedtime fifteen minutes earlier, twenty-five cents off the allowance, no electronic entertainment for two hours, etc.)

Let's imagine the consequence you choose is a rest period or time out. (Time outs work just fine, by the way, if they are administered fairly by non-tantruming adults.) After you say "That's 3, take 5," the child goes to time out. (Some of you are wondering, "How do I get him there?" That question will be answered in the next chapter.)

After the time out is served, you will not believe what happens next. Nothing! No talking, no emotion, no apologies, no lectures, no discussions. Nothing is said unless it is absolutely necessary, which is usually not the case.

Quik Tip...

What is going to happen, in a relatively short period of time, is this: You'll start getting good control—believe it or not—at 1 or 2. And that is going to make you feel real good!

You do not say, for example, "Now, are you going to be a good boy? Do you realize what you've been doing to your mother all afternoon?! Why do we have to go through this all the time? I'm so sick and tired of this I could scream!! Now your sister doesn't behave that way and your father's coming home in half an hour. Did God put you on earth to drive me crazy or what?!"

Tempting as this mini-lecture might be, you simply remain quiet. You practice the proverb that states, " ...a man (or woman) of understanding holds his tongue" (Proverbs 11:12). If the child does something else that's countable, count it. If the child behaves, praise him and enjoy his company.

What is going to happen, in a relatively short period of time, is this: You'll start getting good control—believe it or not—at 1 or 2. You will be helping your children please God because Paul said, "Children, obey your parents in everything, for this pleases the Lord" (Colossians 3:20). And we will promise you this: The first time you stop a fight between two of your kids across fifteen feet of living room, and all you have to do is say, "That's 1" or "That's 2," and you don't have to get up or yell or scream or do something worse which you're going to be sorry about later—the first time you do that, you're going to feel real good!

Some parents ask, "My child always takes us to 2. He never seems to stop at 1. Don't you think he's manipulating us?" The answer is, "No, he's not necessarily manipulating you by always taking you to 2." Why? Because what really drives people crazy is 42 or 72! Or a child who has to be told a thousand times before he'll shape up. Also, remember as Christians we should be merciful. The first two counts are mercy in action: however, there is justice as well. When you get to 3, consequences are administered.

Other parents ask, with good reason, "What if my son or daughter does something so bad that I don't want them to have three chances to do it?" That's a good question. For example, what if your child hits you? Children hitting their parents is unacceptable. If your child hits you, it would be ridiculous to say, "That's 1," and give him two more chances to slug you. So if in your opinion the behavior is bad enough to begin with, you simply say, "That's 3, take 5, and add 15 more for the seriousness of the offense."

Let's look at another example. What if your seven-year-old learns a bad word on the playground? He doesn't know what it means, but he wants to try it out on you. So at 8:30 when you say it's time to get ready for bed, he replies, "You blankity-blank!" Same thing. "That's 3, take 5, and add 15 more for the rotten mouth." And in this example, when that youngster returns from time out, it would be very appropriate to teach the principle found in Ephesians, "Do not let any unwholesome talk come out of your mouths, but only what is helpful for building others up according to their needs that it may benefit those who listen" (Ephesians 4:29). This should not be an extended lecture time, but a short explanation concerning what the word meant and why it is not Christ-like to use it. Explanations are appropriate when a child's misbehavior is new or unusual.

That's it. That's the essence of counting. Counting is extremely simple, direct and effective. You are thinking that there must be a catch. There is.

The Not-So-Easy Part

Occasionally, I have run into parents who say this to me: "We went to your workshop about eight weeks ago and we enjoyed it. We have two fairly difficult kids, aged seven and five. When we went home we were very surprised. *1-2-3 Magic for Christian Parents* worked and our children were much better behaved. But that was two months ago. The 1-2-3 is not working anymore. We need a new discipline program."

Key Concepts...

Talk too much and you take your child's focus off the need for good behavior. Instead, you switch your child's focus onto the possibility of an energetic—and perhaps enjoyable—argument.

What's the problem here? Ninety percent of the time—not all the time—the problem is that the parents "forgot" the No-Talking and No-Emotion rules. Adults can slip up like this without even knowing it. Remember our four-year-old tantrum artist and the potato chips? Here's how that scene might sound if the parent is unwittingly talking too much and getting too excited while attempting to count the child's outburst:

> "That's 1.... Come on now, I'm getting a little tired of
> this. Why can't you do one little thing for us—LOOK
> AT ME WHEN I'M TALKING TO YOU, YOUNG MAN!
> OK, that's 2. One more and you're going to your room, do
> you hear me? I'm sick and tired of you whining and
> fussing over every little thing you can't have. One more and
> that's it. YOUR SISTER NEVER BEHAVES THIS WAY...
> YOUR FATHER'S COMING HOME IN HALF AN HOUR!

OK, ENOUGH! THAT'S 3, TAKE 5. BEAT IT! OUT OF
MY SIGHT!!'"

Whew! What was that? That was a parental temper tantrum. Now
we have two tantrums going on in the same kitchen. This adult's outburst
was not the 1-2-3 at all. What's wrong with what this angry parent just
did? Three things.

First of all, do you want to talk to a child like that? Remember,
"Reckless words pierce like a sword, but the tongue of the wise brings
healing" (Proverbs 12:18). Using reckless words like this parent does
not bring healing. In fact, if you do "communicate" like this parent just
did, the translation of what you are really saying is simply this: "Let's
fight!" And you don't have to have an ADD (Attention Deficit Disorder)
kid or an ODD (Oppositional Defiant Disorder) kid or a CD (Conduct
Disorder) kid—you're going to get a fight. There are plenty of kids who
would sooner cut off their left leg than lose a good battle of words. Un-
wise attempts at talking or persuading are guaranteed to take a child's
focus off the possibility of good behavior and put it on the prospect of
an enjoyable and energetic argument.

Second, many difficult children do have Attention Deficit Disorder.
That doesn't mean they don't *get* enough attention. It means they can't
pay attention. How is an ADD child, or any other youngster for that matter, supposed to pick out—from that huge mass of adult words—the most
important parts, which are the counts or warnings? He can't. Children
can't respond properly to warnings if they don't hear them clearly in the
first place.

Finally, there is a third thing wrong with our super-frustrated parent's
message. Even if you forget all the emotion involved, as mom or dad
talks more and more, their message fundamentally changes. When a
parent gives lots and lots of reasons to a child regarding why he should
shape up, the real message becomes: "You don't have to behave unless I
can give you five or six good reasons why you should, And, gee whiz, I
certainly hope you agree with my reasons." This is no longer discipline.
The word describing this "strategy" starts with the letter B. It's *begging*.
When you beg like this, you are (1) thinking for your child and (2) taking
the responsibility for his behavior.

What's the average child going to do? He's going to take issue with your reasons. "Katie doesn't always do what you say. Daddy's not coming home in half an hour." Now you have left the discipline ballpark and you're out in the street arguing. The main issue has been forgotten. What is the main issue? "Is the child behaving?" is the main issue.

So if the child is acting up, it's "That's 1" (bite your tongue). Then, if necessary, "That's 2" (easy does it, keep quiet), and so on. Remember that the magic is not in the counting, it's in the pregnant pause right after the warning. In that moment—if the adult keeps still—the responsibility for the child's behavior falls squarely on the youngster's own shoulders. You wouldn't want it any other way. Again, the Bible speaks to this principle when it states, "... but a man of understanding holds his tongue" (Proverbs 11:12).

When it comes to counting, your silence will speak louder than your words.

Our Famous Twinkie Example

Our Famous Twinkie Example will help you better understand the workings of the 1-2-3. Here is a situation almost all parents have experienced at one time or another. You are cooking dinner at 5:45 p.m. and your eight-year-old daughter walks into the kitchen:

"Can I have a Twinkie?"
"No, dear."
"Why not?"
"Because we're eating at six o'clock."

Is there anything wrong with this conversation? No. The child asks a clear question and the parent gives a clear answer. The problem, however, is that most kids won't leave it there; they will press the issue further by adding, in a whiny voice, "Yeah, but I want one."

What are you going to do now? You're a little aggravated and you've already given the necessary explanation. Should you repeat yourself? Try to elaborate on your answer? Ignore the child?

Let's play this situation out in three scenes. In Scene I, we'll have starring for us a mother who believes that kids are little adults. Words and reasons will work everything out and change the child's behavior. We'll see what happens with that approach.

In Scene II, our mother will be getting smarter. She will be starting to use the 1-2-3, but the child won't be used to it yet.

In Scene III, the mother will still be using the 1-2-3, and her daughter will have grown more accustomed to it.

Scene I—Starring the Mother Who Believes Kids Are Little Adults:

"Can I have a Twinkie?"

"No, dear."

"Why not?"

"'Cause we're eating at six o'clock."

"Yeah, but I want one."

"I just told you you couldn't have one."

"You never give me anything."

"What do you mean I never give you anything? Do you have clothes on? Is there a roof over your head? Am I feeding you in two seconds?!"

"You gave Joey one a half-hour ago."

"Listen, are you your brother? And besides, *he* eats his dinner."

"I promise I'll eat my dinner."

"Don't give me this promise, promise, promise stuff, Monica! Yesterday—4:30 in the afternoon—you had half a peanut butter and jelly sandwich and you didn't eat anything at dinner!"

"THEN I'M GOING TO KILL MYSELF AND THEN RUN AWAY FROM HOME!!"

"WELL, BE MY GUEST. I'M SICK OF THIS!!"

You can see where trying to talk at the wrong time can get you. Though everything Mom said was true, her talking made things worse.

In the next scene, Mom is getting smarter and starting to use the 1-2-3, but it's new and the child is still getting used to it.

Scene II—Starring the Mother Beginning the 1-2-3:

"Can I have a Twinkie?"

"No, dear."

"Why not?"

"Because we're eating at six o'clock."

"Yeah, but I want one."

"That's 1."

"You never give me anything!"

"That's 2."

"THEN I'M GOING TO KILL MYSELF AND THEN
    RUN AWAY FROM HOME!!"

"That's 3, take 5."

Mom did much better. The temporarily unhappy child disappears for a rest period and the episode is over. How's it going to go when the child is more used to counting and realizes that testing and manipulation are useless?

Scene III—The 1-2-3 After a Few Days:

"Can I have a Twinkie?"

"No, dear."

"Why not?"

"Because we're eating at six o'clock."

"Yeah, but I want one."

"That's 1."

(Pause) "Oh, all right." (Grumpy exit from kitchen)

Good work by Mom again. She doesn't have to count the grumpy "Oh, all right" because the comment is not so bad and the child is leaving the scene of the crime. If the child had said, "Oh, all right, you stupid jerk!" there would be an automatic 3 and the girl would be off to her room for a longer time out.

Is ignoring the child's badgering an option? Perhaps, if (1) the child quickly gets the message and drops the issue and if (2) the parent can stand it. But in general—and especially in the beginning—counting is best.

The Benefits of Counting

There are a lot of benefits to using the 1-2-3 to manage difficult childhood behavior. Here are just a few of them.

Energy savings!

The 1-2-3 will save you a lot of breath—and a lot of aggravation. Parents and teachers say counting makes discipline a whole lot less exhausting. Give one explanation, if absolutely necessary, and then you count. There is no extra talking and no extra emotion. You stay calmer and you feel better—about your child and yourself—when you get a good response at 1 or 2.

Quik Tip...

One explanation—if absolutely necessary—and then you count. You'll save a lot of breath and a lot of aggravation. And when you stay calmer, you feel better—about your child and about yourself.

When is an explanation or more talking absolutely necessary? In those instances when the problem involved is something that the child does not already understand, when what he did is something that is unusual or fairly serious, or when you really need more information from him about what happened.

Here's an example. Your seven-year-old son has been learning trampoline in gym class and he loves it. After school he comes home, takes off his shoes, and attacks the couch in the living room. He's jumping up and down and trying to do flips. You enter the room, see what's going on and are somewhat startled. You say, "That's 1." Your son says, "What did I do?"

Is an explanation in order? Yes. He's never been trampolining on your couch before. You tell him that although he took off his shoes, which you appreciate, you're afraid he'll hurt himself or ruin the couch and that's why you counted.

When is an explanation not necessary? Imagine that a few hours later on the same day, the same seven-year-old—for no apparent reason—gives his younger sister a medium-sized shove right in front of you. You say, "That's 1." He growls, "WHAT DID I DO?!" You say, "That's 2." His response was a defiant and unnecessary question. Do you need to explain that he just shoved his sister? Of course not. There were three witnesses.

An explanation here would invite the boy to argue with you. And this kid sounds like he's ready for an argument! Argue back and you have left the discipline ballpark again.

More time for fun and affection

In the gospel of John, Jesus said, "...I have come that they may have life, and have it to the full." Unfortunately, careless attempts at discipline often prevent families from experiencing the full life Jesus intended. So much time is taken up with discipline that there is not much time left for more positive things. The Talk-Persuade-Argue-Yell—and sometimes Hit—Syndrome can run its course in less than a minute, but it can also occupy hours and hours. During this time everyone is agitated and angry. Parents do not like their kids and kids do not like their parents.

With the 1-2-3, the issue is usually settled in a matter of seconds. Are the children frustrated when they are counted and don't get their way? Of course, but they get over it more quickly than they would if you and they just spent an hour or so trying to persuade, argue and yell each other into submission. After counting, things quickly go back to normal. You can enjoy the full life that Jesus intended with your kids and they can enjoy you. There is not only more *time* for fun and affection, but you also *feel* more like having fun and being affectionate.

Your authority is not negotiable

The Bible clearly gives parents the authority in the home. In Proverbs we find, "My son, keep your father's commands, and do not forsake your mother's teaching" (Proverbs 6:20). In Ephesians we read, "Children obey your parents in the Lord, for this is right" (Ephesians 6:1). You would go crazy if you had to negotiate—every day—issues like getting up, going to school, going to bed, homework, whining and sibling rivalry. You are the boss. As a matter of fact, as a parent you must frustrate your kids on a regular basis, because you can't possibly give them everything they want. But you want to be a nice boss.

Many parents, though, complicate their job of discipline by trying to be too nice and by setting two goals for themselves instead of just one. The first goal is to discipline their children, which is fine. But the second goal is *to get the kids to like it!* Like the mother in Scene I of The Famous Twinkie Example, the parent talks and talks and talks, waiting for the youngster to say something like, "Gee, I never looked at it like that before. Thanks for taking the time to explain it to me. I appreciate your efforts to raise me to be a responsible child."

Let's get real. If your child does listen all the time and more talking seems to help, fine. But with frustrated children that is not usually the case; too often all that talking escalates to arguing and worse. As we have seen before, dozens of verses tout the wisdom of holding your tongue.

The punishment is short and sweet

1-2-3 Magic for Christian Parents does encourage self-control in children, but it also helps *parents* practice self-control. As a parent, it's not easy to be reasonable, especially when you're angry. I saw a mother once who had poured Drano down her four-year-old's throat when the child talked back. I also knew a father who had set fire to his daughter's Cabbage Patch doll in the kitchen sink after a long argument about homework. These are examples of cruel, unusual and stupid punishments.

Though the vast majority of parents will never even come close to taking such ridiculous and nasty measures, they may still be vulnerable to episodes of yelling, name-calling, belittling or even rough physical tactics. These methods go against the admonition found in Ephesians, "Fathers, do not exasperate your children, instead bring them up in the training and instruction of the Lord" (Ephesians 6:4). With *1-2-3 Magic for Christian Parents* the consequences are reasonable, well-defined, and just potent enough to do the job. A rest period or time out lasts approximately one minute per year of the child's life. Time out alternatives might include a quarter off your allowance, a bedtime fifteen minutes earlier, the loss of your game player for two hours, or the successful completion of a brief chore (clean the sink in the bathroom).

These brief and reasonable consequences do not exasperate a child and make him so mad that he wants war. With this regimen, for example, most kids come back from time out having forgotten about the whole thing. And your not being allowed to bring up and rehash what happened — unless absolutely necessary — also helps the house *quickly* return to normal.

Easy for other caretakers to learn

The 1-2-3 is also easy enough to learn that you can train babysitters, grandparents and other caretakers to use it. Parents who are using the 1-2-3 at home often tell their child's teachers about the program. In turn, teachers who use *1-2-3 Magic* in class often share the idea with parents who are struggling with their child's behavior at home.

When kids get the same message from everyone at home and at school, this cross-situation consistency makes the program more powerful and easier for the children to learn. "That's 1" — at home or at school — means "You're doing something wrong and it's time to shape up."

We have found that home-school coordination of the 1-2-3 is especially helpful with behaviorally difficult children. When both parents and teachers use counting fairly and consistently, and when they also respect the No-Talking and No-Emotion rules, we have seen positive revolutions take place in the behavior of some very challenging kids.

Time-Out Alternatives (TOAs)

For various reasons, there may be times when you do not want to use a time out as the consequence for a child's arriving at a count of 3. Perhaps there isn't time for a rest period when you're dashing out the door in the morning, perhaps you feel you want a consequence with a little more clout, or perhaps you want a consequence that fits the crime. The judicious use of time-out alternatives can be of great value.

Here are some TOA possibilities:

Earlier bedtime	Loss of TV for evening
Loss of Gameboy—2 hours	Loss of a toy—rest of the day
No dessert or treat	Monetary fine
No use of phone	Small chore—wash bathroom sink
Larger chore—weed yard	Write a paragraph
No conversation—15 minutes	Removal of DVD, CD player
No friend over	Reduced computer time

Groundings, fines, chores and losses like these can be very useful as consequences, and there are probably many other options. The list of time-out alternatives is limited only by your imagination. Remember to keep the punishments fair and reasonable; your goal is to teach the child something, not to be cruel or get revenge.

Consequences can also be what some people call logical or natural, which means the punishment fits the misbehavior. A child's hitting 3, for example, might mean the end of a pleasant shopping trip. Or a count of 3 might mean the loss of an ice cream bar that was dripping on the car seat. The TV can be turned off if warnings to turn the volume down are ignored. There are obviously many possibilities. Remember when applying natural consequences that kids are still just kids. Exasperated lectures from you, along the lines of "Well, this wouldn't have happened if you'd have simply listened to me in the first place" are unnecessary. Your chattering also interferes with your child's ability to appreciate the connection between his behavior and its consequences.

Getting to the Time-Out Room

If the child won't go to his room after hitting a count of 3, remember you are not allowed to use little adult attempts at persuasion, such as, "Come on now, do what Dad told you. It's only for five minutes and then you'll be able to go back and play. I'm not asking a lot...etc., etc." What you do instead depends on how big you are and how big the child is.

The little kids. Let's say you weigh 125 pounds, and your five-year-old son weighs forty-five pounds. If he doesn't go to his room at 3, you simply move toward him. Some kids will then stay two feet ahead of you all the way to the room. That's OK; they'll soon start going by themselves. Other kids, though, have to be "escorted" (keep your mouth closed while doing this), which can mean taking them gently by the arm, as well as dragging or carrying them—kicking and screaming (that's them kicking and screaming, not you)—to the room. No hitting or spanking. That's if you're 125 pounds and they're forty-five.

The bigger kids. Now let's imagine that it's five years later. Your ten-year-old son at this point weighs ninety-five pounds, and you—through a rigid program of diet and exercise—still weigh 125. You are no longer in a position to be physical with this boy. He's too big, and wrestling matches make a fool out of you and any attempts at discipline.

Your savior here will be the time-out alternative. If after your "That's 3, take 10," the young lad doesn't appear to be going anywhere, you inform him that he has a choice. He can go for time out, or choose one of the following: bedtime will be one-half-hour earlier, fifty cents will come off his allowance, or he can forgo any electronic (including battery-operated) entertainment for the evening. Many parents let the child pick the consequence. If the child refuses, the parent selects the punishment.

A problem arises here, however, because your child hasn't gone to his room and the two of you are still face to face. Lots of kids in this situation want to stick around and argue with you about how stupid your rules are, how stupid *1-2-3 Magic for Christian Parents* is, and how stupid the guys who wrote it must have been. We can't have that.

You know you're not allowed to argue. What are you going to do? You can use a "reverse time out," in which *you* just turn around and leave the room. Go to your room or even the bathroom, if necessary, stock them with good reading materials beforehand, and wait the storm out. Or walk around the house a few times. But don't talk.

Some parents have asked, "Why should I be the one to leave? After all, I'm the adult." Fine. Stay put if you can keep quiet and avoid both being provocative and being provoked. But if your real motive is the desire to stick around for a good fight, that's a bad strategy.

Bringing up children in the training and instruction of the Lord is a difficult assignment. *1-2-3 Magic for Christian Parents* is one tool that can help. The 1-2-3 method is certainly very straightforward, but managing kids' irritating behavior is never an easy job. At this point you probably have a few questions about this first big phase of parenting. Let's take a look at some of the most important and frequently asked ones.

Points to Remember...

The Benefits of Counting

1. Energy savings
2. More time for fun and affection
3. Your authority is not negotiable
4. The punishment is short and sweet
5. The 1-2-3 is easy for other caretakers to learn

Questions for Christian Practice

1. Read Proverbs 15:5 and Philippians 2:14-15. How should children respond when they are disciplined?

2. If someone were to ask you why talking can interfere with discipline, how would you respond?

3. Describe a situation with your child where you might have to go straight to 3 and add additional time.

4. List some potential Time-Out Alternatives that you think would be effective with your child.

5. How do you plan to use the extra time and energy you save by using 1-2-3 Magic?

6
Twenty Questions

Blessed is the man who finds wisdom, who gains understanding.

Proverbs 3:13

1. What do you do if the child counts you back?!

Your five-year-old is whining at you because you wouldn't take her to the pool on a hot summer day. You look at her, hold up one finger, and say, "That's 1." She looks back at you, holds up one tiny finger, and says, "That's 1 to you, too!"

What should you do? Oddly enough, this common occurrence sometimes throws even the most confident parents for a loop. They are at a loss how to handle the unexpected rebellion.

The answer is very straightforward. Your kids do not have the authority to count anyone (unless you give that power to them). The child might as well have said, "The moon is made of cream cheese." The comment means nothing.

If the child's remark appears to be a humorous attempt to tease you a little, you can just ignore it. If her "That's 1 to you, too!" however, is sarcastic and disrespectful, count it by simply holding up two fingers and saying nothing. If the child again mocks your response, she will have just arrived at 3.

2. What if there's an obvious problem between the children, but you didn't see what happened?

Your daughter, Suzie, comes running into the kitchen and yells, "Dad, Bobby should get a 1!" You haven't the slightest idea what the problem is, but the chances are the issue revolves around sibling rivalry. In general our rule is this: If you didn't see the argument or conflict, you don't count it; if you hear it, you can count it.

If you're in the kitchen and you hear a ruckus starting in the family room, for example, there's nothing to stop you from calling, "Hey guys, that's 1." Of course, you want to use this rule with flexibility. If you feel one child is consistently being victimized by another, you may have to intervene and count just the aggressive child. On the other hand, if the tattling is getting out of hand, many parents decide to count the tattler.

3. How long do you take in between counts?

About five seconds. Just long enough to allow the child time to shape up. Remember that we're counting Stop (obnoxious) behaviors, such as arguing, whining, badgering and teasing, and for obnoxious behavior it only takes a child one second to cooperate with you by stopping the annoying activity. We certainly don't want to give a child half an hour to continue a tantrum before giving him a 2.

Counting is perfectly designed to produce the one second's worth of motivation necessary for cooperation. We give the kids five seconds, though, which is a little more generous. Why five seconds? Because this brief pause gives the youngsters time to think things over and do the right thing. In those few seconds — provided the adult keeps quiet — kids learn to take responsibility for their own behavior.

4. If a child hits a 1 or a 2, does he stay at that count for the rest of the day, even if he does nothing else wrong?

No. The time perspective of young children is short. You would not say "That's 1" at nine in the morning, "That's 2" at 11:15, and "That's 3, take 5" at three in the afternoon. So we have what we call our "window of opportunity" rule: If a six-year-old, for example, does three things wrong in a thirty-minute period, each warning counts toward the total of three. But if he does one thing wrong, then an hour goes by, then he does something else he shouldn't, you can start back at 1.

Very few children manipulate this rule by doing one thing, allowing thirty minutes to pass, and then figuring, "Now I get a free one!" If you feel a youngster is trying to get away with this, simply make the next count a 2 instead of going back to 1.

The window of opportunity should be longer as kids get older, but there are no hard-and-fast guidelines. For four-year-olds the time period might be only ten or fifteen minutes, but for eleven-year-olds it might be two to three hours.

5. My child has a fit when I try to drop him off at preschool. No matter how much I try to reassure him, he screams whenever I try to leave.

Though separation anxiety is normal in little children, the kids' desperate screams when you try to leave them at preschool, with a sitter or even at grandma's can be very upsetting to you. Here's what you do. Bite your upper lip and become the Master of the Quick Exit. When dropping children off (or leaving home), kiss the kids goodbye, tell them when you'll see them again and get out of there! The longer you stay and the more you talk, the worse you will make everything.

If these awful moments make you feel like a totally cold and uncaring adult, call back later and ask whoever the caretaker is how long your child cried. The average is eighty seconds.

6. Does the room have to be a sterile environment?

No. Many books tell you the time-out room should be modeled after a cell in a state penitentiary. Complete and utter boredom—that'll teach 'em! This is unnecessary. The child can go to the room and read, take a nap, play with Legos, draw and so on. She doesn't even have to stay on her bed. Just to be safe, though, there are three things that are forbidden: no phone, no friends and no electronic entertainment.

Some people ask: "Well then, just how is a rest period supposed to work? My kid tells me that time out's fine with her—she doesn't care and she'll just go upstairs and play." Don't pay much attention to any child who says, "I don't care." That comment usually means the opposite: She does care. And if her room were such a great place to be, she would have already been up there.

The fact of the matter is, the power of the 1-2-3 does not come so much from the time out itself; it usually comes from the interruption of the child's activities. It just so happens that when this girl was timed out for hitting her brother, she was watching her favorite TV show, *Garfield*. Now she has to miss a big chunk of the show. No one—including you—likes to be interrupted so you miss out on something fun.

If you really feel the time out is not effective, consider three things. First, are you still talking too much and getting too emotional during discipline efforts? Parental outbursts ruin everything. Second, if you feel you are remaining calm and time out is still not working, consider another time-out place or room. Third, consider time-out alternatives.

Quik Tip...

Don't forget—you can count different misbehaviors to get to 3. That's a lot easier on your aging memory bank. And if mom gives a 1, dad can follow it up with a 2. The 1-2-3 works a lot better if the kids know both parents are going to count when necessary.

7. Can you count different misbehaviors to get to three?

Yes. You don't have to have different counts for each different kind of misbehavior. Imagine: "Let's see, he's on a 1 for throwing that block across the room. He's on a 2 for teasing his sister. He's on a 1 for yelling at me. He's on a 2 for..."

This routine would soon drive you insane and you'd need a personal computer to keep track of everything. So if the child pushes his sister, for example, "That's 1"; throws a block across the room, "That's 2"; and then screams at you for counting him, "That's 3, take 5." The child is gone.

Mom could say 1, dad could say 2 and mom or dad could say, "That's 3." In fact, we encourage you to share the joy. Actually, it's better if mom and dad *do* both count, because then the kids know that both parents are behind the plan—they are consistent and really serious. The involvement of both parents makes it easier for the children to shape up. In the same way, the involvement of both home and school in doing the 1-2-3 also makes it easier for kids to behave—especially the really difficult children. Difficult kids really need consistency across situations.

8. Can you ever ignore anything?

Yes, but don't ignore a lot in the beginning. *In the beginning, when in doubt, count!* After a while, when you're getting a good response at 1 or 2, you may be able to let up a little. Let's say, after a few weeks of getting used to the 1-2-3 program, your child does something right in front of you that would normally be counted. Instead of counting right away, just watch your youngster. The child can almost "feel" the count coming. Sometimes, if you say nothing, the child will spontaneously exercise self-control and stop the misbehavior. This response is ideal, because now the child is internalizing the rules and controlling himself without direct parental intervention. Isn't that the kind of person you want to drop off at the dorm on the first day of his freshman year in college?

How do you know when you should count? It's not too difficult to tell. Most of the time, if you're irritated about something and that something is a Stop behavior, you should be counting. Just to be sure, you can also write yourself a list (or do it with your spouse) of countable behaviors and then show it to the kids. Some parents and teachers even have the children help make up the list.

The question of ignoring certain types of behavior leaves room for some variation among parents. Why? Because some parents simply have longer fuses than others. Some parents, for example, will ignore kids' rolling their eyes, stomping off, grumbling and whining, while other parents will count. Some parents will ignore a child's yelling or even pounding walls as long as he's on his way to time out. Other parents will lengthen the rest period for that kind of behavior. Either strategy is correct if it is done consistently. You have to clearly define what kinds of child behavior, in your well-considered opinion, are too obnoxious, too rude, too aggressive or too dangerous. Then make up your mind that those behaviors are the ones that will be counted.

9. What if you have other people over?

By this time, you can probably anticipate the answer to this question. You will need to (1) get used to counting in front of other people and (2) not alter your strategy one bit when others are watching. The ultimate test, of course, is when you're out in public (see next chapter). For right now, we'll discuss what should happen in the safety of your own home.

From time to time, other people will be at your home when your kids decide to act up. In fact, the presence of other people often seems to trigger disruptive behavior in many kids, presenting parents with a complicated challenge: disciplining children while on stage. Among the groups of people who perversely decide to put you in this awkward position are other kids, other parents (with or without their kids), and, finally, grandparents. Let's examine the problems presented by each group.

Other kids. If your youngster has a friend over, count your child just as you would if no one else were there. If your child gets timed out, he goes to the room and—remember—his friend may not join him. Just explain to the other boy or girl that you're using this new system and his buddy will be back in five minutes or so. If your son or daughter says to you, as some have, "Mom, it's so embarrassing when you count me in front of my friends," you say to them once, "If you don't want to be embarrassed, you can behave."

Another thing you can do in this situation is count the other child too. After all, it's your house. If his parent is there, though, you'd better ask permission and explain a bit before you go disciplining her child.

Another variation, with other kids over, is "1-2-3, 1-2-3, 1-2-3: out of the house to play." This can be very helpful, especially if you have a difficult child who often gets overly excited when a playmate is over. With this routine, at the third time out, instead of sending your child to the room again, both kids must now leave the house for a specified time (assuming the weather isn't nasty) and play outside. This variation of the 1-2-3 is very popular in southern California.

Or—even better—1-2-3, 1-2-3, 1-2-3, then send them over to the other kid's house to play!

Other adults. If you have other adults or other parents over at your home, you will probably feel considerably more nervous counting your child in front of these grownups. This discomfort is normal. Although you may feel a little self-conscious at first, you'll soon get used to do-ing the 1-2-3 under these circumstances. So count! If you don't take the plunge, your children will sense that you are much easier prey when other people are around.

On the other hand, when you count in front of another parent, something surprising may happen that you will enjoy. You're talking to a friend and your child rudely and loudly interrupts you demanding a snack. You calmly say, "That's 1." Your child not only quiets down, she also leaves the room. The other parent looks at you like, "What did you do?!" Just tell her about the 1-2-3 and explain how it works. This type of scene, by the way, is one of the major ways that *1-2-3 Magic* gets passed around.

Grandparents. For our purposes here, there are three types of grandparents, whether you're visiting them or they're visiting you. The first—and rarest—type of grandparent is the *cooperative* grandparent. She will count along with you. You say 1, Grandma says 2, and so on. That kind of cooperation is super, but it doesn't happen as much as we'd like.

Like the first type, the second type of grandparent is also nice to have around. This person we call the *passive* or *unintrusive* grandparent. This grandma or grandpa leaves you alone when you're disciplining the kids and doesn't interfere. That's often not easy for a grandparent.

The third type of grandparent, however, is the *antagonistic* grandparent. He will say something to you like this: "You have to read a book to learn how to raise your kids?! Why, when I was a boy, all Dad had to do was look at his belt...." You know the rest. The message is that you don't need any of this modern, psychological stuff.

A second kind of antagonistic grandparent will actually interfere with your discipline. You say to little Bobby, "That's 3, take 5," and before he can move, Grandma butts in and says, "Oh, little Bobby didn't really do anything. Bobby, come and sit on Grandma's lap for a while."

Some parents ask at this point: "Can you count the grandparents?" Probably not, but you do have an assertiveness problem on your hands. You may have to say something like, "You know, Mom, I love you very much, but these are our kids and this is the way we're raising them. If you can't go along with the agenda, the visit may have to be cut short a little." Although this statement will be a very difficult one to make, the comment will definitely be an investment in your children's future.

Can you imagine saying that to your parents?!

10. Can you use a time-out chair instead of a room?

You can use a stair or a chair for a time out (don't use a corner of the room), but only if the child does not make a game out of the situation. Some kids, for example, sit on the chair at first, but then start gradually losing contact with it. Eventually they may just be touching their little finger to the chair and looking at you like, "What are you going to do about this?" If your rule for time out is simply that the child must stay in contact with the chair, this is no problem. Just don't pay any attention to the youngster. But if the child is getting on and off or away from the chair and you're uncertain what to do, this kind of game will ruin the discipline.

We usually prefer that visual contact between parent and child be broken during the rest period, so the child can't tease or provoke you. That's why the child's bedroom or other safe room is preferable. Many parents, however, have successfully used stairs and chairs and many report that the kids—even some wild ones!—sit still on them, don't talk and don't keep getting off. As a matter of fact, parents are often very creative in coming up with places for time outs.

11. Can you use counting for toilet training?

No. Counting is not especially effective for potty training. One reason is that if you are trying to count children's messing their pants, you don't always know the exact moment when the "accident" occurs, and so you don't know just when to count. In addition, most experts agree that punishing kids for wetting or soiling is not particularly helpful.

Though there are several effective ways to get kids to go on the toilet, my favorite method is for the parent to do very little formal training. Too many parents are in too big a hurry to get their kids potty trained, and this big rush can cause all kinds of trouble. Instead let the kids see you use the toilet and get them a potty chair of their own. Most children will eventually learn how to use the thing without much direct coaching from you. When they are successful, you can then praise and reward them.

Another frequently unsuccessful parent tactic in this regard is repeatedly asking a child—when he's looking squirmy—if he has to go to the bathroom. It's much better to say this: "Some day you're gonna surprise me and go on the potty!"

12. What if the child won't stay in his room?

Many kids will stay in the room for time out, even if the door isn't shut (it doesn't have to be shut). Others, however, will try to keep coming out. With very small children, one alternative is to just stand there blocking the way or to hold the door shut. After a few time outs the kids get the idea that they can't come out. This tactic won't work, however, if you keep getting into major tugs of war with the door. Once again, if your discipline comes down to this level, you look stupid and so does your approach.

A second alternative is to block the child's exit with the kind of gate that squeezes against the door jambs. These gates can be used as long as the children are not able to either climb over or knock down the device. Yet another option is to start the time out over if the child comes out prematurely. Some parents will then double the time of the second rest period. This method, of course, won't be much help with two- or three-year-olds because they won't understand, but with older children it can work well. Explain once and then start.

Some kids, however, are so rambunctious that they just keep coming out and accumulate what seem like thousands of extra time-out minutes. What should you do? You need to secure the door in some way or another. There are several options.

Some parents of difficult children, believe it or not, have made the child's bedroom door into a "Dutch" door. They saw the door in half, then lock the bottom part and leave the top part open during the time out. You may think that's a pretty drastic solution. It is, but some kids require drastic (but gentle) solutions.

Also available are plastic door knob covers. These devices cover the knob and have to be squeezed tightly enough to be able to turn the knob and open the door. Many young children aren't strong enough to accomplish this feat. Another idea is to simply put some kind of lock on the door. This advice worries some parents, who think that their child will become claustrophobic or that locking the door is abusive. Locking the door by itself is not abusive, but for some parents (foster parents) and in some places it is illegal. If you have a really difficult child, you should check into what regulations hold for your situation and get some professional advice.

Here's the deal with locking the door. You tell your child that as long as he stays in his room, the door will remain open or simply shut. But the first time he comes out, the door gets locked for the rest period. Many children will quickly learn to stay put without the door having to be locked. If you still prefer gates to locks, purchase one of the more solid gates that bolts into the door jambs. If the child can climb over the gate, get a taller one or put two up.

The main point is this: Some children, including many of our Attention Deficit (ADD) friends, will try to keep coming out of the room. Securing the door in some way or another is absolutely essential. It is totally unproductive and harmful to be chasing the kids back in the room all the time; the child must know that the door is a barrier that he's stuck with for a short time. If you worry about the safety of the child, childproof the room, secure any windows and remain outside the door during the time out, but try not to let the child know you're there. And don't forget the one-minute-per-year rule for the length of the rest period. Remember that you may not increase the length of the time out simply because you're in a bad mood. You can increase the length of time out—to a point—if the child did something that is exceptionally bad.

Once children learn they can't get out of the room, they will stop tantruming and calmly accept the brief period of quiet.

13. What if the child won't come out?

You probably know the answer to this one: Relax and enjoy yourself! You go to the bedroom door and say, "Time's up." Your son or daughter replies, "I'm never coming out again as long as I live!" Don't say, "Good!" or anything like that. Just walk away—never chase a martyr.

On the other hand, do not cheat by inadvertently extending the time out. Imagine your child's time out was for five minutes. You just noticed, though, that you had gotten distracted and eight minutes have elapsed. You think, "Oh, it's so peaceful! And she's being so quiet in her room! I don't have the heart to let her out." Wrong—no fair. Keep an eye on the clock or timer, then tell the child when the time is up. If your girl has fallen asleep—and if it's OK for her to nap at this time of day, let her snooze for a bit.

Some kids always want a hug and some reassurance when time

out is over. What do you do? Give them a hug! But be careful with these little huggers. If a child repeatedly requests a hug, you'd better check to make sure you're doing the 1-2-3 correctly. Some kids, of course, are just very sensitive and any kind of discipline upsets them a little. Other children, however, need reassurance because you were too harsh—emotionally or physically—before you sent them to the room. So if you get a little hugger, make sure you're gently following the No-Talking and No-Emotion rules.

14. Help—my kids go nuts when I'm on the phone!!

This question brings back vivid memories to all parents. It seems that there are no parents in the entire world whose children don't act up when the parents are on the phone. Lots of kids start running around and screaming as soon as the infernal device rings.

At our house the dog would also get into the act. The phone would ring and the dog would bark. The dog's bark was a signal to the kids, "We've got another victim on the line, get down here and let's torture them for a while!" Then they'd all be running around, yelling and barking and having a wonderful time. Whoever was on the phone, though, would feel trapped and frustrated.

Why does it seem that children always act up when you're on the phone? At first I thought it was because the kids were jealous because their parent was talking to someone else and ignoring them. There may be some of this feeling, but now I believe the main reason is that the youngsters think you are *helpless*. The kids seem to believe that since your head is attached to the phone, you won't be able to do anything to counter their raising a ruckus.

What you do is count the children just as you would if you weren't on the phone—much like when you have other people over. While you're on the phone you have somebody else present—but only listening, not watching. You may have to interrupt your conversation to count. You may have to put the phone down, explain what you're doing to the person you're talking to, or even hang up so you can escort a little one to her room. Long distance calls can become more expensive, but whatever it takes, do it. Otherwise the children will know that you are a sitting duck every time someone calls and you'll get the royal treatment.

This phone routine is not easy in the beginning. After a while, though, many parents succeed in training the children to the point where the adults don't have to say anything while counting. They simply hold up the appropriate number of fingers while they continue their conversation! And the children respond because they know Mom or Dad means business. If you have gotten to this point, it's a mighty handy tactic to use when you're talking on the telephone.

15. Does being counted hurt the child's self-esteem?

Most kids aren't counted a lot, so the mere quantity of counts is usually not a problem. Once you've gotten started at home, many children will not get any counts for days at a time.

For those children who do get counted more often, if you are doing the 1-2-3 correctly, there should be no significant threat of hurting self-esteem. What *will* hurt youngsters' self-esteem is all the yelling, arguing, name-calling, belittling, sarcasm or hitting you may do if you don't control yourself and do the program right. In addition, as you will see later, your overall feedback to your children should be much more positive than negative. And one count is one bit of negative feedback. Therefore, you will want to more than balance off your occasional counting with other activities or strategies, such as affection, shared fun, active listening and praise.

16. What if the kid wrecks the room during his so-called "rest period"?

By far, the vast majority of children will not be room wreckers. Only a small percentage of kids will throw things around and mess up the room. An even smaller percentage of children will break things, tear their beds apart or kick holes in the wall. These kids do exist, however, and their parents need to know how to handle these sometimes scary actions.

The whole point behind *1-2-3 Magic* is that parents be ready for anything, rather than feeling defensive and worrying, "Oh no, what is he going to do now?" We want your attitude and message to the children to be something like this: "You're my child and I'm your parent. I love you, and it's my job to train and discipline you. I don't expect you to be perfect, and when you do do something wrong, this is what I will do."

The credit for the solution to the room-wrecking problem comes from a couple who visited my office a long time ago. They had an eight-year-old boy who was very nice to me in my office, but—according to his Mom and Dad—"hell on wheels" everywhere else. These parents said they were thinking of putting this boy's name on their mail box, because it felt like he was running the house. They often referred to their son as "King Louis XIV."

This behavior obviously couldn't go on, so I asked these parents if they wanted to learn *1-2-3 Magic*. They said yes. I taught them the program, prepared them for testing and manipulation and they went home to get started. This boy had been used to running the house—but little did he know, when his parents got home they were ready for him.

When King Louis hit 3 for the first time, he could not believe what happened. How his parents got him to his room for his first "rest period" is still a mystery, but when he got there, he totally—and I mean totally—trashed the place. His first tactic, and perhaps the favorite of all room wreckers—was to empty his dresser and throw his clothes all over the floor. Then he ripped the blankets and sheets off his bed. Next he pushed the mattress and box springs off the bed frame. Then he proceeded to his closet, took out all his hanging clothes, and one by one threw them all over the room. After that, all his toys were flung out of the closet. Finally, he went to the window and tore down his curtains.

What did his parents do? Amazingly, they never called. The first thing they did was nothing! They didn't clean up the mess or have King Louis clean it up. Any cleaning up would only have meant loading the boy's gun again for the next time out: another perfectly neat room to wreck. Second, Mom and Dad continued to count their son aggressively but fairly. When the young lad earned a 3, he got a 3 and a consequence. No fudging around with fractions such as, "That's 2-and-a-half, that's 2- and-three-quarters, or that's 2-and-nine-tenths." The parents would just hit him with his well-earned 3 and then send him to his bedroom to rearrange the trash. When bedtime came, this boy had to find his pajamas. He also had to find his bed. In the mornings, his clothes for school didn't match for a week.

How long did it take for King Louis to learn that there was new management in the old maison? It took about ten days for him to start calming down during time out. Then, after three or four days of peaceful time outs, his parents helped him clean up his room. After that—believe it or not—he hated to be counted, and his parents would stop him on a dime with a count of 1.

Key Concepts...

Most parents will not have children who wreck the room during time out. But those moms and dads who do better be ready! Don't be intimidated—they're just kids. And be sure to follow our simple rules.

Now, did we break this boy's spirit? Was he now going to be an eternal marshmallow for the rest of his life? Certainly not. Now he was really and consistently the nice kid I had seen in the office, and his parents were in charge of their own house as they should have been. In addition, the boy started behaving better in school, where the teacher was also using the 1-2-3.

If you think you are going to have a room wrecker, before starting the 1-2-3 check out two things. If there is anything dangerous or harmful in the room, or anything valuable that can be broken, take it out before the first "rest period." For example, if the child has a hammer and a saw in the room, or if Grandma has her Hummel collection on top of his dresser, get those out of there before you start counting.

17. Room wrecking is one thing, but what do you do if your child urinates on the floor during time out?

Some kids have done it—usually preschoolers. You send them to time out and they are so mad, they pull down their pants and cut loose. What do you do? You time them out to the bathroom.

I know what you're thinking: "How naive! Do you really expect the youngster to use the facilities appropriately?" The answer is "No, we don't expect the youngster to use the facilities appropriately." That's not the point. The point is this: What's easier to clean, the bedroom rug or the bathroom floor? If the child goes on the bedroom rug, cleaning is an expensive project. If the child goes on the bathroom floor or the smaller bathroom rug, it's a different story.

The same advice holds true if you have one of these children who can get himself so upset that he throws up. In every workshop I've ever done, there are a few parents who have kids like this. Make sure the bathroom's safe, then time him out to the bathroom.

18. Should you ever spank a child?

Let's face up to reality: *ninety-nine percent of all spankings are parental temper tantrums*. They are in no way attempts to train or educate a child. They are simply the angry outburst of a parent who has lost control, doesn't know what to do and wants revenge by inflicting pain. Parents who have big problems with self-control and anger management try to justify and rationalize spanking by saying things like, "You have to set limits," "It's for their own good," and "Having to hit the kids hurts me more than it does them."

But doesn't the Bible teach that if you spare the rod, you will spoil the child? The verse in question is Proverbs 13:24. The Amplified version puts it this way: "He who spares his rod (of discipline) hates his son, but he who loves him disciplines diligently and punishes him early." The emphasis in this verse is less on the method of discipline and more of an admonition *to* discipline. Consider a similar verse, "Discipline your son, and he will give you peace; he will bring delight to your soul" (Proverbs 29:17). Again, the Bible is emphasizing the wisdom of discipline, not necessarily the use of corporal punishment. There may be parents who judiciously—without tantruming themselves—utilize corporal punishment with younger children; however, the 1-2-3 plan should make this unnecessary.

We realize that some Christian parents disagree, feeling that spanking is condoned by the Bible, is effective, and may also be the way they were raised. If you are considering using spanking as a disciplinary tool, consider the following thoughts beforehand:

1. Way over 95% of spankings are parental temper tantrums rather than sincere training efforts.
2. If you are totally honest with yourself, can you say that you never enjoy spanking as an act of revenge?
3. Spanking should never be a first option; it should always be a last resort.
4. Spanking should never be repeated blows or full force.

5. If spanking is becoming a regular occurrence at your house, consider a psychological evaluation for child and parents.

Remember, the whole point of the 1-2-3 program is to avoid the Talk-Persuade-Argue-Yell-Hit routine.

19. Why three counts? Children should respond the first time you ask! Why give the kids three chances to misbehave?

1-2-3 Magic is an interesting phenomenon. Some people think counting is too dictatorial, while others see counting as a sign of parental weakness.

The reason for three counts is simple: you want to give the kids two chances—the first two counts—to shape up (unless what they did was so serious that it merited an automatic 3). Remember our job is to train our children, "Train a child in the way he should go, and when he is old he will not turn from it" (Proverbs 22:6). How are children going to learn to do the right thing if they never get a chance? And with counting, the "chance" comes right away—in the first few seconds following the count. That immediate opportunity helps them learn good behavior.

20. Shouldn't the kids ever apologize?

This is a tough question. If you're currently asking the kids to apologize, and that routine is working well, fine. Keep in mind, however, that many apologies are really exercises in hypocrisy. Requiring an apology is often simply part of the child's punishment—not a learning experience involving sorrow or compassion.

For example, your two sons have gotten into a fight. You break up the tussle, then demand that they apologize to one another. The older boy glares at the younger, and with a sneer on his face says, "I'm sorry." His tone is forced, begrudging and sarcastic. Was this a real apology? Of course not. His comment was merely a continuation of the original battle, but on a verbal level. *His comment was also a lie*. These two may be slugging it out again as soon as your back is turned. If you want to insist on apologies, make sure that you are not simply asking your children to lie.

Have we taken care of all possible questions? Not quite. The most commonly asked question needs a whole chapter devoted to it: *What do you do in public?*

Questions for Christian Practice

1. Read Proverbs 5:23, 10:17 and 15:32. What are the results of not heeding discipline?

2. Which question/answer in this chapter was the most helpful? Explain.

3. How do you plan to handle discipline when you're on the phone or when other people are over?

4. What positive changes do you hope to see after beginning the 1-2-3 plan?

5. What other questions do you hope to have answered as you read the rest of the book?

7
What to Do in Public

*Let us not become weary in doing good, for at the proper time
we will reap a harvest if we do not give up.*

Galatians 6:9

We now must come to grips with the worst nightmare of every
parent: what to do in public. No one wants to look like a child
abuser in aisle 5, the candy aisle, of the local grocery store. And kids—even
very young toddlers—seem to have radar that can sense psychological
vulnerability in anxious parents.

Once they have learned the mechanics of the 1-2-3, many parents
worry about being out in public where there is no time-out room. Believe
it or not, this problem can be solved without too much difficulty. That,
my fellow parents, happens to be the good news. The bad news is that
there is a worse problem lurking in the shadows, and deep in her heart
every parent knows what that problem is.

Your biggest problem is that your little ones can hold something
over your head in public that they can't hold over your head in private:
the threat of public embarrassment. This fear of embarrassment and
public disapproval has at times made even the most competent parents
forget what they're supposed to do, change their tactics and crumble. Try
to remember these two basic principles: First, the long-term welfare of
your kids comes before short-term worries about what others are going

to think. And second, remember that our ultimate goal is to please God with our parenting and not others. The Bible states, "Man looks at the outward appearance, but the Lord looks at the heart" (1 Samuel 16:7b).

Counting in Public

Let's imagine that you do have a five-year-old and that yes, in fact, aisle 5 in the grocery store, the candy aisle, is one of your biggest problems. It seems as though every time you go down that aisle, your son asks for candy, you say no because all the candy bars are huge, and then the little boy proceeds to throw a ferocious tantrum. He throws himself on the floor, screams at the top of his lungs and—don't you love this part?—a crowd has gathered to see how you're going to handle the crisis.

What do you do? The first thing you do is make sure you have the 1-2-3 rolling fairly well at home. "Fairly well" means you are getting a good response at 1 or 2 most of the time. Why not all the time? Because he's just a kid.

Now you're in aisle 5, your son is tantruming loudly, and the audience has assembled. You look down at the unhappy little monster, hold up one finger and say, "That's 1." You say this as calmly and as firmly as you would at home. What is the key here? The key is not so much what you do as what you don't do. You do not, for example, let yourself be intimidated by the threat of public embarrassment and whisper, "Come on now, I don't want you making a fool of me in front of all these people." You do that and the child will *know* that you can be had for a nickel; he won't need the candy bar because he's about to have more fun with you.

Proceed to 2 and then to 3, if necessary. Do not look at anyone else other than your child. At this point, of course, parents wonder, "What are we going to do at 3? There's no time-out room." This problem is easier to solve than you think.

Time-Out Room, Time-Out Place

Over the many years of developing the *1-2-3 Magic* program, parents taught us what to do in situations like this. These were parents who, in the heat of battle, had to come up with rest-period solutions while in the restaurants, in the theaters, in stores, at the museum, at the ball park and at church on Sunday.

We call the solution, "Time-Out Room, Time-Out Place." *When you are out, there is always either a room, something like a room, or a symbolic place where a time out can be served.* For example, in the grocery store, at 3 some parents will just stay right where they are and hold the child's hand for several minutes. The adult says nothing during this period. That's a time out place. Other parents have put little children in the grocery cart for the consequence. That's something like a time-out room.

Quik Tip...

When you're out in public, there is always either a room, something like a room, or a symbolic location where a time out can be served. And don't forget your time-out alternatives. Just because people are watching does not mean that you have to be at your kids' mercy!

Other ideas include a corner of the store (a time-out place). For more rambunctious children, the bathroom of the store can serve the same purpose. Let them scream their heads off in there for a while. Some parents, feeling their children play up to an audience, will actually leave the grocery cart right where it is and take the child back to the car to do the rest period. That's like a time-out room.

Using the car like this makes some people ask, "Why should I have to go through all that trouble?" The answer is because (1) they're just kids, (2) they're still learning how to behave and (3) "all that trouble" is a sound investment in their future and your peace of mind.

Here's another idea. If the child is old enough and you won't worry about him, at 3 have him wait for you—perhaps next to one of the cash registers or next to the information booth—till you're done shopping.

During any time out, you do not talk to the child. No lecturing, screaming or nagging. Keeping quiet is often very hard, but after a while the youngsters get the idea you mean business. And yes, there have been parents who felt the fuss was bad enough that they left a half-full grocery cart and went home.

The "1-2-3-4"

Don't forget your Time-Out Alternatives (TOAs) when you have to go out of the house with the kids! Here's another situation. You're cooking a new recipe for dinner and you are so excited about this new dish that you can hardly stand it. At 5:15 p.m., however, you suddenly realize you are missing three essential ingredients. To make matters worse, your six-year-old and eight-year-old are in the other room playing well together for the first time in two-and-a-half years. You're going to have to interrupt them and there's no time to get a sitter.

Here's what you do. Tell the kids that you have to go shopping, it will take about an hour and they have to go with you. You know they don't want to, but you're all stuck. Tell them the deal will be this: If they're "good" while you're out (meaning they don't hit a count of 4—you're giving them an extra count because of the length of the trip and because they don't want to go), you'll buy them a treat. Their reward will be $1 cash or $1 worth of whatever else they may want to buy. If they hit the count of 4 during the trip, however, the reward is gone.

Some parents feel this is bribery. It is! The wisdom of Proverbs says "a bribe is a charm to the one who gives it..." (Proverbs 17:8). But the real definition of bribery is paying someone to do something illegal. Here we're paying the kids to do something legal, and it works.

My wife and I had a very interesting experience using this TOA tactic with our kids when we used to go out for ice cream in the evening. The first few times we went out for our after-dinner treat, the kids fought like cats and dogs in the back seat. By the time we all got our ice cream, no one was in any kind of a party mood anymore.

So one evening I told the kids this: "Guys, we're going out for ice cream. But there's going to be a new deal. If you guys hit a count of three before we get there, we turn right around and come home. Nobody will get any ice cream."

With hopeful hearts, we took off in the car. The children started fighting. I said,"That's 1, third count blows the trip." Sure enough, they were soon at 2, and then, only half way to the ice cream store, they hit a 3. I turned the car around and went home. The kids were not pleased; they looked stunned and resentful.

A few days later—this time less hopeful—we took another shot at an ice cream outing. We weren't three hundred yards from the house when the kids started fighting again. I said,"That's 1, third time blows the trip." They hit a 2 and then a 3, and the car got turned around again.

I'm sure that before our next attempt at an evening treat the kids had had a conversation with each other. Their conversation probably went something like this: "Isn't it a shame that most children in the world, except us, have normal fathers? Unfortunately, our Dad turned out to be a shrink. But he's got the car and he's got the money, so if we want some ice cream, we'd better put up with his stupid games!"

So, about a week later, our intrepid group once again set out on its quest. To my amazement, the kids started fighting. I said, "That's 1, third time blows the trip." To my further amazement, however, the kids instantly became quiet and they were good as gold the whole rest of the way. We all enjoyed our dessert.

One moral of this story: Sometimes it takes a few trials for you to make believers out of the kids. By the way, I've often been asked what to do if while on the way one child acts up and the other one doesn't. The answer: The one gets the ice cream and the other one doesn't. But don't expect to enjoy the ride home.

Keep Moving

Another tactic that parents have used successfully in public takes us back to our grocery store example, where the youngster was having a major fit in the candy section of aisle 5. What some parents have done is simply leave the child on the floor and move on to aisle 6. When they meet someone in aisle 6, they say, "Boy, do you hear all that racket over there?"

Seriously, what often happens is that the child starts worrying where mom or dad went, forgets the candy and runs to find his parent. Naturally, you wouldn't want to get too far away, depending on the age of the child. Then again, some kids run to find their parent and then remember the candy and continue the tantrum. What should you do then?

The answer to this question depends on two things: How badly do you need to shop and how much guts do you have? A number of years ago I was shopping by myself in our local grocery store. I saw a lady come in with a four-year-old boy. She picked the boy up, put him in a cart and pushed the cart past the bubble-gum machine. The boy asked for gum, the mother said no and the boy went ballistic. The mother kept moving and said nothing.

I shopped for twenty minutes, this Mom shopped for twenty minutes, and this little boy howled for twenty minutes. Wherever you were in the store, which was not large, you could hear this kid's blood-curdling screams. But this lady was great. She paid no attention to her son. She had come in for milk, green pepper and converted rice, and she was going out with milk, green pepper and converted rice. I remember passing this duo in the rice aisle. While the youngster wailed, his mother was calmly looking at the rice box: "Let's see, four ounces times six. Yes, that should be enough for tonight."

I was impressed. But Mom was soon to fall off her pedestal. I hurried along because I wanted to get out of this noise-filled place. I got to the check-out line. The racket behind me started getting louder. Here they come! This lady and her unhappy son got in the next line, and she checked out sooner than I did because she had fewer items. With great relief I watched her leaving the store, with her son still tantruming. As she passed the bubble-gum machine for the second time, she stopped and bought her son a piece of gum!

I was dumbfounded. I almost lost all my professional decorum right there. I wanted to jump over the counter, run up to this woman, and say, "Excuse me, maam, you don't know me, but I'm a clinical psychologist. Could I talk to you for a moment?" This mother had just rewarded a twenty-minute tantrum.

There may be times out in public when, in spite of everything you've done, your child won't stop a tantrum. Your choices then are these: Gut it out and finish your shopping (you will feel foolish), take the child out to the car until he does stop screaming, or go home.

Going To Church

Taking your children to church is a great family activity, but it can also be very challenging both to you and those sitting around you. Practicing some of the principles we've just discussed can make for a more worshipful and fulfilling experience.

Many churches provide childcare or a children's service. These are great options giving your child a more age appropriate setting to participate in. However, if the situation calls for your family to be together, prepare your child. Let her go to the restroom and get a drink of water before the service begins. Consider bringing paper, pencils, or colors for younger children. You can encourage her to draw pictures of parts of the service to keep her involved. Older kids can take notes on the service. This activity can help the youngsters stay focused and it also gives you a basis for later discussions.

You will find Time-Out Alternatives (TOAs) are useful when you are in church. Let your kids know that 1-2-3 will be in effect and what the TOAs will be. (Time-out itself may not be such a good choice for a consequence since your child may welcome the chance to change environments).

The 1-2-3-4 is also a good method to use. Offer the kids a positive reward if they don't reach 4 during the service. For younger children you may choose a graduated system of implementation. Let them stay in the service for a short period of time to begin with and then increase the length week by week.

Church should be a positive experience. You will have a much better chance of enjoying the service by having a specific plan and preparing your children for it in advance.

Don't Take Them Unless You Have To

Have you ever been to church on Sunday, and in the row ahead of you there is a couple with a two-year-old? The two-year-old, of course, isn't paying any attention to the service. Neither are his parents, since they are preoccupied with trying to keep their son in line so he won't bother other people. Finally, around this family trio are ten other individuals who aren't paying any attention to the service either, because they're busy evaluating how well the couple is disciplining their two-year-old.

So, in effect, we have thirteen people who might as well have not gone to church at all. In this situation the church nursery would have been a better option for the child, as well as for everyone involved. Don't ask for unnecessary trouble in public by putting your kids in situations they simply can't handle. With the two-year old above, even though the parents are trying their hardest not to allow their son to bother the other people around them, these other people are being distracted anyway.

Riding in the Car

Travelling in the car is a kind of half-public, half-private experience which can present parents with some extremely difficult and even dangerous situations. Travelling parents often feel like an unwilling captive audience to their children's misbehavior. And making matters worse, moms and dads also know their discipline options are limited.

Have you ever been riding along an interstate with your left hand on the steering wheel while your right hand is waving madly through the back seat trying to grab the kid who's just been teasing his sister for the fifty-seventh time since you left the last town? Vacations are supposed to be fun, but this kind of routine is not fun. I've had many parents tell me that they pretty much stopped taking vacations because of nasty and repeated scenes like these.

Counting is very useful when chauffeuring the kids around town. The question, of course, is what to do at 3. Time-out alternatives are one choice. One couple, for example, didn't allow anyone to talk—including Mom and Dad—for fifteen minutes after the kids hit 3 for behavior like teasing, fighting or badgering. Other families have used fines (money taken off the allowance), at the rate of about five cents for each minute that would have been included in the child's normal time out.

You can also do an old-fashioned time out. Where is the time-out room? You're riding in it! Your car is actually a stylish, gas-guzzling time-out room. Over the years a very effective tactic for many of my parents was 1-2-3, then pull the car off to the side of the road for the rest period. This strategy is dramatic and has quite an impact on the children.

For some reason, counting the kids in the car and having them serve the time outs when they get home doesn't work as well, unless you're very close to home. The problem may be that the rest period comes too long after the offense. In addition, the demand for a time out when you walk in the door may simply start another fight, because often by the time you get home everybody has forgotten the original problem.

On longer car rides and on vacations, counting can also be used effectively, just as it is with short trips. But other tactics are often helpful. Other tactics that parents have used successfully in the car include the usual—and very helpful—activities like the alphabet game and car bingo. Putting one child in the front and one in the back has been useful, as has using a VCR or DVD player (and renting twenty movies!) or leaving at 4:00 in the morning so the kids sleep away the largest part of a four- or five-hour ride. Telling the kids they get fifty cents for every goat they see is also a brilliant maneuver.

The main point is this: Don't ever leave on a car ride with the kids — or especially on a long "vacation" — without putting on your thinking cap first. Have the 1-2-3 and a few other tactics in your hip pocket, because you're going to need them.

Points to Remember...

Even though it's not easy, the long-term welfare of your children should come before your short-term worries about what other people are going to think of you as a parent. So when you're out of the house with the family, be prepared and stick to your guns!

Questions for Christian Practice

1. Read Galations 1:10, 1 Thessalonians 4:1, Proverbs 29:25. What does the Bible say about being overly concerned about man's opinion?

2. Describe a time when your child misbehaved in public.

3. How have you handled misbehavior in public and in your vehicle?

4. What is your biggest concern about using the 1-2-3 in public?

5. Describe how you plan to handle taking your kids out after you begin the 1-2-3 plan?

8
Variations: Sibling Rivalry, Tantrums and Pouting

How wonderful, how beautiful, when brothers and sisters get along!
Psalm 133:1 The Message

Three common but aggravating childhood problems require a few minor modifications in our counting procedure because of their unique natures. The first issue involves sibling rivalry, which many parents put at the top of their List of Hugely Aggravating and Repetitive Behavior Problems. The other two behaviors are temper tantrums and pouting.

Sibling Rivalry

When you have more than one child acting up, your life has just become more complicated. There are more actors in the drama. How are you going to handle the situation? There is no need to make things more complex than necessary. Here are a few simple and important rules that you should follow:

Count both kids. When the children are fighting, you should count both kids most of the time, because *usually* they both helped produce the conflict. Kids are tricky; some provoke in subtle ways and others in more aggressive ways, so it is often hard to tell who started a fight—even if you are right there.

For example, have you ever been driving in the car with the kids in the back and you hear, "Mom, he's looking at me again!"? Who started that one? There's really no way to tell. So you count both children, unless one is the obvious, unprovoked aggressor and you're absolutely positive.

Never ask the world's two stupidest questions. Every parent knows what these questions are: "What happened?" and "Who started it?" What do you expect to hear, a version of George Washington's "I cannot tell a lie"? "Yes, I started this fight and the last thirteen consecutive squabbles have also been my personal responsibility." That kind of confession won't happen. Instead, all you get is the kids blaming one another and yelling.

> **⚠ CAUTION**
>
> Never ask the world's two stupidest questions: "Who started it?" and "What happened?" unless you think someone is physically injured. Do you expect your kids to come up with George Washington's version of "I cannot tell a lie"?

There are, of course, times when you might need to ask what happened. If, for instance, you think someone might be physically injured, you would want to examine the child and find out what caused the injury. The same thing might be true with other serious or unusual cases. But for your run-of-the-mill sibling rivalry, trying to find out what happened is too often a lost cause.

Don't expect an older child to act more mature during a fight than a younger child. Even if your two kids are eleven years old and four years old, don't say to the eleven-year-old, "She's only a baby; can't you put up with a little teasing?" That comment is the equivalent of loading the gun of the four-year-old, who will be sure to both appreciate your generosity and to take maximum advantage of it.

Along these same lines, imagine for a second that your eleven-year-old son comes up to you one day and says, "I want to ask you a question."

"Go ahead," you say.

"How come I always get a ten-minute time out, and Miss Shrimp over there (your four-year old) only has to go for five minutes?"

"Because the rule in our house," you say, "is one minute of time out for each year of your life."

"WELL THAT'S THE DUMBEST THING I EVER HEARD OF!"

"That's 1."

This child doesn't really want information. He wants a fight. Remember your authority is non-negotiable. The Bible clearly states, "Children, obey your parents in everything, for this pleases the Lord" (Colossians 3:20). Don't get sidetracked into a useless argument. With *1-2-3 Magic* we have a rule that goes: Count attacks and discuss discussions.

What if the kids have a fight and they share the same room? It would not be a good idea to send two fighting children to the same time-out place to continue their fight. Send one to his room and the other to an alternate time-out room or place. Then for the next rest period reverse the locations. Or use time-out alternatives when both children fight. If your kids have separate bedrooms and they fight on the way to their rest periods, extend the time outs by five or ten minutes.

Temper Tantrums

Let's say your son got timed out for tantruming. He's now in his room and he's still having a fit. The problem here is simple: What if the time-out period is up but the child's not done with the tantrum? You don't want to let him out in his condition and, in a sense, he's just earned another time out. The answer to this dilemma, fortunately, is also simple: The time out doesn't start until the tantrum is over. So if it takes the youngster fifteen minutes to calm down, the rest period starts after fifteen minutes. And if it takes the kid two hours to calm down (could be a room-wrecker), the time out starts after two hours.

And don't be sticking your head in there every five or ten minutes saying things like, "Come on now, don't you think that's enough? We miss you. Dinner's in five minutes and you have homework to do...." Just leave him alone until he's tired of being angry.

The only children we don't use this temper-tantrum modification for are the two- and three-year-olds. They don't seem to get the idea, so just let them out after a couple of minutes, even if they're still tantruming, and cross your fingers. Once they're out, ignoring the child is usually more effective than trying to talk him out of his irritation. If he still doesn't quiet down, leave him in a little longer the next time.

Pouting

Pouting is a passive behavior that is designed to make you feel guilty. If you do wind up feeling guilty when your child pouts, that's really more your problem. Why should you feel bad for trying to be a good parent? The Message puts it this way, "Discipline your son (or daughter), for in that there is hope; do not be a willing party to his death" (Proverbs 19:18). According to this passage, if you don't discipline your child you could be hastening his demise. In Hebrews we find, "No discipline seems pleasant at the time, but painful. Later on, it produces a harvest of righteous and peace for those who have been trained by it" (Hebrews 12:11).

So if you discipline a child and she gives you the ultimate in martyr looks, just turn around, say nothing and walk away. The only time you would do something different is if you get what we call an "aggressive pouter." An aggressive pouter is a child who follows you all over the house to make sure you don't miss a minute of the sour face. If she does that, "That's 1." She's trying to rub your nose in her grumpiness, and you're not going to allow her to do that.

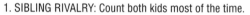

Points to Remember...

1. SIBLING RIVALRY: Count both kids most of the time.
2. TEMPER TANTRUMS: The time out doesn't start until after the tantrum is over.
3. POUTING: Pouting can be ignored unless the child becomes an "aggressive pouter."

Questions for Christian Practice

1. Read the following passages; John 13:24 and Ephesians 4:29. What is the long-term goal for your family relationships?

2. Describe a specific conflict between your children? How did you handle it?

3. How can implementing the 1-2-3 help with your children's sibling rilvary?

4. Does your child throw temper tantrums or pout? Describe these behaviors.

5. How will you handle tantrums or pouting now that you know the 1-2-3 plan?

9
The Kickoff Conversation

Children, obey your parents in the Lord, for this is right.
Ephesians 6:1

Getting started with the 1-2-3 is pretty easy. The Kickoff Conversation, in which you explain the new regime to the children, only takes about five to ten minutes. Even though it's a bit like a little-adult-type explanation, you should give the kids the benefit of the doubt and tell them what you'll be doing. But don't put a lot of stock in the impact of this initial conversation. Wishful thinking on your part will not do the job. Lots of children don't really get the idea until you've been counting for a while and they've been to their rooms a few times.

If both parents are living at home, or even if mom and dad live in separate places, it's preferable if both grownups sit down together with the youngsters and do the initial explaining.

Here's what you say:

"Listen, you guys know there are times when you do things we don't care for, like arguing, whining and teasing. From now on we're going to do something a little different. When we see you doing something you're not supposed to, we'll say, 'That's 1.' That's a warning, and it means you're supposed to stop. If you don't stop, we'll say, 'That's 2.' That will be your second warning. If you still don't stop, we'll say, 'That's 3, take

5 (or however many minutes equals your age).' That means you have to go to your room for a time out or a kind of rest period. When you come out, we don't talk about what happened unless it's really necessary. We just forget it and start over.

"By the way, kids, there's part of this new system that you'll like and part you won't like. Here's what you won't like: If the thing you do is bad enough to start with, like swearing or hitting, we'll say, 'That's 3, take 10 or 15.' That means there aren't any other warnings, you just go straight to your room, and the time will be longer.

"The part you will like is that most of the time we won't talk about what happened after a time out. Well, that's the new deal. It's pretty simple. Do you have any questions?"

You could also share a verse like the one at the beginning of this chapter. "Children obey your parents in the Lord." You might want to offer a prayer asking God to help your children grow in obedience. Keep the Kickoff Conversation brief and to the point; it is not time for a sermon. Remember the principle found in Proverbs 29:19; "Children cannot be corrected by mere words."

The Children's Reaction

Expect the kids to sit there and look at you like you've just gone off your rocker. Some kids will poke each other and exchange knowing glances, as if to say, "Well, it looks like Mom went to the library again and got another one of those books on how to raise us guys. Last time she stuck to it for about four days, and Dad never did anything different at all. I think if we stick together and hang tough, we should be running the house again inside of a week, right?"

Wrong. Don't expect the children to be grateful, to look enlightened or to thank you for your efforts to raise them responsibly. Just get going, stick to your guns and—when in doubt—count!

What about two- and three-year olds who won't understand an initial explanation? You have

> **Quik Tip...**
>
> Don't expect the children to thank you or look enlightened after the Kickoff Conversation. Some kids will be puzzled and others won't believe you're serious. You'll soon make believers out of them, though, by your consistent, gentle and decisive follow-up.

two options. Just start counting and doing time outs. Little kids are much smarter than we often give them credit for. They'll get the idea quickly.

Or, if two parents are living at home, try a little role playing. Dad pretends he's acting up, say by whining or yelling. Mom firmly counts dad with a 1. Dad continues his misbehavior, so he advances to 2 and then 3. Mom sends dad to his room for a time out. Father cooperates but looks a little grumpy. The kids giggle. The children won't giggle when you start counting them, but the role play will help them get the idea.

At this point of this book, you may feel that you're ready to start using the 1-2-3. Not so fast! If you began counting right now, you wouldn't be prepared for the fact that many children—about half—are going to give you a hard time in the beginning. That may be the bad news, but the good news is that we're on to the youngsters now! We have discovered and identified the Six Kinds of Testing and Manipulation. Once you understand these tactics and what's behind them, you'll be ready for anything.

Points to Remember...

You are almost ready to begin your first giant parenting step:

Controlling Obnoxious Behavior!

Questions for Christian Practice

1. Read James 1:22-25, Matthew 7:21. How important is it to put God's word into practice?

2. Describe any concerns you have about beginning the 1-2-3 plan.

3. Plan your Kickoff Conversation. Include where and when you will meet and what you will say.

4. How do you think your children will respond?

5. What do you look forward to most about having better control of your children?

Part III

No Child
Will Thank You

10

The Six Kinds of Testing and Manipulation

Do everything readily and cheerfully—no bickering, no second-guessing allowed!

Philippians 2:14 The Message

It is important for parents to take a long-term view of parenting. The verse for the very first chapter of this book was this: "Train up a child in the way he should go, and when he is old he will not turn from it" (Proverbs 22:6). The wise writer of Proverbs was reminding parents of the long-term consequences of their parenting style. In order to help children develop good character for the future, parents cannot give children everything they want. In addition, parents must train their kids to start doing things the children don't want to do (homework, going to bed) and stop doing some things they do want to do (teasing, whining). Parents who are able to accomplish these goals will help their children develop the character necessary for success as adults.

Unfortunately, children are not always grateful for good parenting. Though most children learn to tolerate discipline and to understand that it will help them in the future, children will still engage from time to time in what we call testing and manipulation. Testing and manipulation are the efforts of the frustrated child to get what he wants or to avoid discipline by getting his parent emotionally confused and sidetracked. Three things need to be remembered about testing:

1. Testing occurs when a child is frustrated. You are not giving him the potato chips he wants; you are counting him; you are making him do homework or go to bed. He doesn't like this and hopes for a way to get what he wants in spite of your efforts.

2. Testing, therefore, is purposeful behavior. The purpose of a child's testing, obviously, is to get his way rather than have you impose your will on him. In fact, testing and manipulation can have two purposes; the second goal often appears if the first goal is frustrated:

1. The first purpose of testing and manipulation is for the child *to get what he wants*.

2. The second purpose of testing kicks in if the first purpose is not achieved. If the child cannot get his way, he will try to get something else: *revenge*.

3. When engaging in testing and manipulation, a child has a "choice" of six basic tactics. All six can serve the first purpose: getting one's way; five of the six tactics can serve the second purpose: revenge. Usually a child's testing behavior will represent a combination of one or more of the basic tactics.

> **Key Concepts...**
>
> The first goal of testing is for the child to get what he wants. Since he's less powerful than you are, he must use some emotional manipulation. If the child still fails to get what he wants, the second goal of testing is often revenge.

All parents and teachers will quickly recognize the manipulative tactics we are about to describe. These adults have encountered these ploys of children many times. Grownups are also usually aware—if they think about it—of which maneuvers are used by which children. Moms and dads may also recognize some of their own favorite strategies, since adults use the same basic manipulative methods.

By the way, the use of testing and manipulation does not mean that a child is sick, emotionally troubled or in need of psychological care. Attempts to get your way, as well as attempts to "punish" the bigger people who don't give you your way, are perfectly normal. The use of testing also does not require an exceptionally high IQ. In fact, adults are often amazed at how naturally and how skillfully little kids are able to produce, as well as modify, complex testing strategies. Because our sons and daughters are so naturally skilled, it is very important that adult caretakers understand children's testing and how to manage it.

The Six Basic Testing Tactics

Here are the six fundamental strategies that children use to attempt to influence the adults who are frustrating them:

1. Badgering

Badgering is the "Please, please, please, please!" or "Why, why, why?" routine."Just this once! Just this once! Just this once! Just this once!" "Mom! Mom! Mom! Mom! Mom!" There are some children who could have been machine guns during World War II. The child just keeps after you and after you and after you, trying to wear you down with repetition. "Just give me what I want and I'll shut up!" is the underlying message.

Badgering can be particularly taxing when it is done very loudly and also when it is done in public. Some parents attempt to respond to everything the frustrated child says every time she says it. Mom or dad may try to explain, to reassure or to distract. As badgering continues, though, parents can become more and more desperate, going on the equivalent of a verbal wild-goose chase — searching for the right words or reasons to make the youngster keep quiet. Many kids, however, are extremely single-minded once their badgering starts. They won't stop until they either get what they want or until their parent uses a more effective approach to stop the testing. We'll soon clarify exactly what that approach will be.

Badgering is what we refer to as a "blender" tactic, since it mixes easily with other manipulative strategies. The basic element in badgering, of course, is repetition. So when any of the other verbal testing tactics are repeated again and again, the resulting manipulative strategy is a combination of that other tactic plus the repetitive power of badgering.

2. Temper (Intimidation)

Displays of temper, or what we sometimes refer to as intimidation, are obvious, aggressive attacks. Younger children, who aren't so adept with words yet, may throw themselves on the floor, bang their heads, holler at the top of their lungs and kick around ferociously. Older kids, whose language skills are more developed, may come up with arguments that accuse you of being unjust, illogical or simply a bad parent in general. When frustrated, older kids may also swear or angrily complain.

Some children's fits of temper go on for very long periods. Many ADHD and bipolar children, for example, have been known to rant and rave for more than an hour at a time. In the process they may damage property or trash their rooms. Tantrums are often prolonged (1) if the child has an audience, (2) if the adults involved continue talking, arguing or pleading with the youngster or (3) if the adults don't know what to do.

Temper fits in two-year-olds can be aggravating, but they can also be funny. My wife took a picture of our son when he was an energetic toddler having a temper tantrum right in the middle of the ashes in the fireplace at my parents' home (the fire was not going, of course). We all can still laugh at that scene.

As kids get older and more powerful, however, tantrums get more worrisome and just plain scarier. That's why we like to see them well controlled or eliminated by the time a child is five or six.

3. Threat

Frustrated kids will often threaten their parents with dire predictions if the adults don't come across with the desired goods. Here are a few examples:

> "I'm going to run away from home!"
> "I'll never speak to you again!"
> "I'm going to kill myself!"
> "I'm not eating dinner and I won't do my homework!!"
> "I'm going to kill the parakeet!"

The message is clear: Something bad is going to happen unless you give me what I want immediately. Give me the Twinkie right before dinner, stop counting me, don't make me go to bed, OR ELSE! Some of the threats that younger children come up with are funny. One little girl, whose mother was trying to get her to go to bed, angrily shouted, "All right, I'll go. But I'm going to lie there all night with my eyes open!"

Another six-year-old boy was reprimanded and timed out by his father for squirting the dog with a hose. The boy threatened to run away, actually packed a small bag and walked out the front door. After five minutes, however, he walked back in the door and yelled at his dad,"I couldn't run away because you guys won't let me cross the street!"

Other threats are not funny. Some frustrated children threaten to kill themselves, and this is something no parent takes lightly. Parents wonder if this is just manipulative or if their child really wants to die. Two questions can help parents sort out this dilemma. First of all, is this child generally happy? Does she enjoy life most of the time, have friends, do OK in school and fit into the family? If the answers to these questions are positive, it is less likely that the child wants to end her life. Second, did the suicidal threat come out of the blue or was the comment a response to some obvious, recent frustration? If "I'm going to kill myself" comes out of nowhere, the threat is always more worrisome and needs to be looked into.

4. Martyrdom

Martyrlike testing tactics are a perennial favorite of children. When using martyrdom the child may indicate that his life has become totally unfair and an incredible burden. "No one around here loves me anymore," "I never get anything" or "You like her more than me" are examples.

Or the youngster may actually do something that has a self-punitive, self-denying flavor, such as not eating dinner, sitting in the closet for an hour or staring out the window without talking. Crying, pouting and simply looking sad or teary can also be effective manipulative devices.

The goal of martyrdom, obviously, is to make the parent feel guilty, and martyrdom can be surprisingly effective. This testing tactic is very difficult for many adults to handle. Many moms and dads seem to have a "guilt button" the size of the state of Wyoming! All the kids have to do is push that button and the youngsters wind up running the house.

Children learn early on that parents are highly invested in the welfare of their offspring. Kids know their caretakers want them safe, happy and healthy. Unfortunately, kids also seem to naturally appreciate a logical consequence of this adult commitment: Acting hurt or deprived can be a powerful way of influencing adult behavior.

Two-year-olds, for example, will sometimes hold their breath till they turn blue when they are mad about not getting what they want. Many parents wonder how a child can even come up with an idea like that. Another creative child, whose mother had just sent her to her bedroom, was heard yelling out her window, "I can't breathe! I can't breathe!" This tactic may have been creative, but it was not effective.

What's Going On Here?

Before we finish our list of the Six Kinds of Testing and Manipulation, let's stop and figure out what this commotion is all about. Just exactly what are the kids trying to accomplish with all these maneuvers, and how do they think the process will work?

Quik Tip...

Remember that a child who is testing you is offering you a deal: Give me what I want and my badgering, temper, threat or martyrdom will end—immediately! Does that sound like a deal you can't refuse? Accept it and you're in trouble.

Most kids, of course, would never be able to describe the underlying mechanics of testing. But we can tell you *exactly* what's going on. Here's how it works: The first four tactics—badgering, intimidation, threat and martyrdom—share a common dynamic. The child, without quite knowing what he's doing, is in effect saying to the parent something like this: "Look, you're making me uncomfortable by not giving me what I want. You're making me get out of bed, you're counting me for teasing my sister or you're not buying me a treat.

But now I'm also making you uncomfortable with my badgering, tantrums, ominous statements or feeling sorry for myself. *Now that we're both uncomfortable, I'll make you a deal: You call off your dogs and I'll call off mine."*

If you give in and give the child what he wants, you are guaranteed that any testing will stop immediately. In a split second, no more hassles. However, we find these instructions for good parenting in I Timothy, "He must manage his own family well and see that his children obey him with proper respect" (I Timothy 3:4). This applies equally to fathers and mothers. If you give in to your children's testing, who's managing your family? It certainly isn't you: it's the kids. God has given the parents charge of the family, not the children. Giving in to manipulation transfers a parent's God-given authority to the kids.

Now let's finish our list of testing tactics. The last two, when compared to each other, are like day and night.

5. Butter Up

The fifth tactic, butter up, takes an approach that's different from the first four. Instead of making you feel uncomfortable, with butter up the child tries to make you feel good. You may then run the risk of losing this good feeling if you subsequently frustrate the child.

"Gee, Mom, you've got the prettiest eyes of anybody on the block" is a fairly blatant example. Or, "I think I'll go clean my room. It's been looking kind of messy for the last three weeks. And after that maybe I'll take a look at the garage."

With butter up the basic message from child to parent is: "You'll feel really bad if you mistreat or discipline or deny me after how nice I've been to you." Butter up is intended to be an advance set-up for parental guilt. The child is implying, "You'll feel so positively toward me that you won't have the heart to make me feel bad."

Promises can be used by children as butter up manipulation. "Please, Mom. Please. I'll eat my dinner and I promise I won't even ask for any dessert," said one little girl who wanted a snack at 5:00 in the afternoon. Some promises kids make are impossibilities. One little boy, while in the process of pressing his father for a new computer said, "I'll never ask you for anything ever again."

Apologies can be sincere, and they can also be examples of butter up testing. "I'm sorry, I'm sorry. I said I'm sorry," one little boy pleaded in an attempt to avoid a grounding for socking his little brother.

Butter up manipulation is obviously the least obnoxious of all the testing tactics. Some people, in fact, don't think it should be labeled as testing at all. It is true that butter up is sometimes hard to distinguish from genuine affection. If a child says "I love you" and then proceeds not to ask for anything, it's probably genuine affection. And a child who asks if he can have a friend over if he cleans up his room may be proposing a straightforward and legitimate deal. But if you've ever heard a parent say, "The only time my son's ever nice is when he wants something," that person is probably referring to butter up.

6. Physical Tactics

From a parent's perspective, this last form of testing is perhaps the worst strategy of all. Here the frustrated child may physically attack an adult, break something or run away. Physical methods of trying to get one's way, of course, are more common in smaller children who don't have well developed language skills. When the use of this type of testing continues beyond age four or five, however, we begin to worry. Some kids have a long history of this kind of behavior, and the bigger the child gets, the scarier their physical strategies get.

Some parents who use time outs, for example, tell us that their children sometimes physically attack them when the parent is trying to escort the child to the time-out area. (Any child who is mad enough to assault his parent is certainly not going to go voluntarily to his room.) Some youngsters become quite ferocious, kicking, biting, scratching, pinching and hitting while yelling at the top of their lungs.

Other frustrated, physically-oriented kids will smash or break things—sometimes even their own possessions. One ten-year-old boy, for instance, was sent to his room for fighting with his brother. The door to his bedroom happened to be shut when he got to it, so he gave it one of his best karate kicks, cracking the door down the middle. Another lad smashed a coffee mug on the tile floor in the front hall of the house. Unfortunately, one of the larger pieces of the mug went flying into the glass storm door, which promptly disintegrated.

Another physical testing tactic, running away, is not used a lot by younger children. Threats to run away appear more often in this age group. One seven-year-old boy, though, used a different version of this idea on his mother, who had just denied his request to go outside. The boy sneaked down to the basement and hid for two hours, not respond-ing to anyone who called his name. The tactic was effective, at least in punishing his mother, who was beside herself with worry by the time her son reappeared.

Badgering, temper, threat, martyrdom, butter up and physical tactics. These are the methods children use to get their way from adults. And all these tactics, except butter up, can also be used by kids to punish the uncooperative adults who obstinately persist in refusing to give the youngsters what they want.

Which strategies are the favorites of your sons and daughters? We have taken several surveys of parents and teachers, asking which tactics they thought children used the most. Interestingly, both groups of grownups always mention the same three: badgering, temper and—the overwhelming favorite—martyrdom.

You will also be interested to know that the most annoying manipulative maneuver used by children is a tactic that combines two of the above three favorites. This tactic, which drives many parents absolutely nuts, is a combination of badgering and martyrdom. The word describing the behavior starts with the letter W. You guessed it: Whining!

Who's Pushing Your Buttons?

Now we're going to ask you a very important question. Think of each of your kids, one at a time (if you're a teacher, reflect on each of your students) and ask yourself, "Does this child have a favorite testing tactic? One that he or she uses very frequently or all the time?" If your answer is yes, that's bad.

Why? Because the testing ploy *works* for the youngster. People don't generally repeat behavior that doesn't work for them.

What does "works" mean? All you have to do is recall the two purposes of testing and manipulation. First of all, a testing strategy works when the child successfully gets his way by using that tactic. How do you know if a child is getting his way by testing? It's obvious—you just give it to him. You give him the snack right before dinner, turn the TV back on while he's

> **CAUTION**
>
> Does your child have a favorite testing tactic? If your answer is yes, that's bad. It's bad because the strategy is working for the youngster, either by getting the child her way or by getting her effective revenge.

doing homework, stop counting him when he's teasing the dog or don't make him go to bed.

"Works" can also refer to the second purpose of testing and manipulation: revenge. Children will repeat tactics that provide an effective way of retaliating against the adults who are causing the frustration. How does a child know if she is effectively getting revenge? The answer takes us right back to the No-Talking, No-Emotion Rules. If this child can get you very upset and get you talking too much, she knows she's got you.

Some kids retaliate by making their parents angry. The youngsters know they are getting effective revenge when their parents start talking like this: "How many times do I have to tell you!" "Why can't you just take no for an answer!!" "ARE YOU TRYING TO DRIVE ME NUTS!!!" The angry part of your frustrated child will find comments like these satisfying, and the next time your child is angry with you, he will know exactly how to press the revenge button.

You want some homework done, for example, and your son has a tantrum (Tactic #2) because he wants to watch TV. Your response, however, is a *counter* temper tantrum. You get more upset than your son did! Final score: Child 5, Parent 2. He got you: The small, inferior part of the youngster got the angry big splash from the larger, "more powerful" adult.

Other kids retaliate by making their parents feel guilty. Imagine that your daughter—when asked to go to bed—resorts to martyrdom (Tactic #4): "Well, it's obvious that nobody around here loves me anymore. I might as well hitchhike to the next state and find a family more compatible with my basic needs" (she adds a touch of threat, Tactic #3). You feel frightened and guilty. You are certain that unloved children grow up to be mentally ill, homeless or serial killers. You sit the youngster down on your lap, and for a half hour tell her how much you love her, how much Dad and the dog love her, and so on.

You have just been had by Tactic #4, Martyrdom. You are squirming and uncomfortable, and your child is making you pay for your parenting sins. Always remember this: Unless you are a grossly neglectful or abusive parent, your kids know that you love them. By all means tell them that you love them, but never tell them that you love them when they're pulling a #4 on you.

How to Manage Testing and Manipulation

Since you are a Christian, the Holy Spirit will provide you with some resources that will be necessary in facing testing and manipulation. "But the fruit of the Spirit is love, joy, peace, patience, kindness, goodness, gentleness and self control..." (Galatians 5:22-23). You will need the peace, patience and self-control the Spirit provides to stand firm.

Now let's say you're getting into the flow of *1-2-3 Magic for Christian Parents* and you're toughening up some. Your ten-year-old son wants to go to a friend's house at 9:00 on a school night. You deny his request and tell him it's too late. The following scene occurs:

"Why not? Come on, just this once!" (Badgering)

"Can't do it."

"I never get anything." (Martyrdom, Badgering)

"I don't think you're too underprivileged."

"I'll clean the garage tomorrow." (Butter Up, Badgering)

"The garage is OK the way it is. I just cleaned it."

"This stinks—I HATE YOUR GUTS!" (Intimidation, Badgering)

"Sorry."

The child throws a book on the floor. (Physical Tactic)

"Watch your step, pal."

"Please, PLEASE! Oh, come on, it's not so late." (Badgering)

"No way. Not tonight."

"If you don't let me, I'm running away!" (Threat, Badgering)

This may be aggravating, but in a way it's good! Why? Because something constructive is happening. The child is fishing around, switching tactics and probing for your weak spot. *But he can't find a weak spot.* You are sticking to your guns. Not only that, you are remaining fairly calm in spite of the aggravation.

There is one thing wrong with this example, however, and that has to do with how you handle testing. You would not let the child switch tactics that many times (and you would also not talk so much). What should you do, then? Well, if you look at our list of six testing tactics, five of them (except butter up) are Stop behavior. Stop behavior should be counted. So if a child were pushing you this much, he would be counted.

This is how the scene above should be handled if you were using the 1-2-3. Remember that the boy has already been given an explanation:

"Why not? Come on, just this once!" (Badgering)
"That's 1."
"I never get anything." (Martyrdom, Badgering)
"That's 2."
"I'll clean the garage tomorrow." (Butter Up, Badgering)
"That's 3, take 10."

The third count is more for the badgering than the butter up, but it's obvious this kid's not going to give up until the parent gently but firmly puts her foot down. That goal is achieved by counting.

Remember: With the exceptions of butter up and passive pouting, testing and manipulation should be counted, especially in the beginning when you're just starting *1-2-3 Magic*. Once the kids are used to the discipline system, the less aggressive, less obnoxious forms of testing can—at your discretion—occasionally be ignored. The effectiveness of not responding at all (verbally or nonverbally) to a child's testing can be evaluated by how quickly the child gives up the battle. Many kids will quickly learn that no response at all from you (ignoring) means that this time they are not going to either get their way or get effective revenge.

What to Expect in the Beginning

As we mentioned before, once you start counting, the kids will fall primarily into two categories: immediate cooperators and immediate testers. Immediate cooperators you simply enjoy. You will feel more affectionate toward your youngsters because they are listening to you. You will want to have more fun with your kids, talk with them, praise them and listen to them. You will enjoy working on building a good relationship. This good relationship, in turn, will make counting (1) less necessary and (2) a lot easier when it is necessary.

Immediate testers, however, get worse at first. When you let them know you're going to be the boss and you take away the power of their favorite testing strategies, these children deteriorate in two ways. Some will *up the ante* with a particular testing tactic. The volume and length of a child's tantrums, for example, may double. Badgering may become more intense or aggressive, and martyrdom may become more whiney and pathetic.

The other unpleasant change you may see initially in noncooperators is *tactic switching*. The kids may try new manipulative strategies you've not seen before, or they may return to others they haven't used for years. The most common switches involve going from badgering and martyrdom (and whining!) to temper. Some kids, quite understandably, blow up when their attempts to wear you down with repetition or make you feel guilty fail. Although tactic switching is aggravating, remember that switching is almost always a sign that you are doing well at sticking to your guns. Keep it up!

What do you do when faced with tactic escalation and tactic switching? Several things are important: (1) Don't get discouraged; this is a normal stage children go through while adjusting to *1-2-3 Magic*. (2) Count when necessary. (3) Keep your mouth shut except for necessary explanations and the counting itself. Eventually tactic escalation and tactic switching will diminish and your youngsters will accept your discipline without having a major cow every time you have to frustrate them. You then have won the battle. You are the parent, they are the children and your home is a more peaceful place.

One final word: Some kids, after cooperating initially, become "delayed testers" later on. Delayed testing can occur after the novelty of the new system wears off, when the youngsters begin to realize that they aren't getting their way anymore, or if your routine gets disrupted by travel, visitors, illness, new babies or just plain time.

If you're unprepared for it, delayed testing can be a bit disillusioning. You think to yourself, "The kids were so good before!" You may feel like the whole system is falling apart, or that it was too good to be true. Fortunately, the remedy is not far away. Read *1-2-3 Magic* again, watch the video, discuss the suggestions with your spouse if possible, then get back to basics: No Talking, No Emotion, be gentle but aggressive and when in doubt, count. Things should shape up quickly.

Points to Remember...

The Six Kinds of Testing and Manipulation

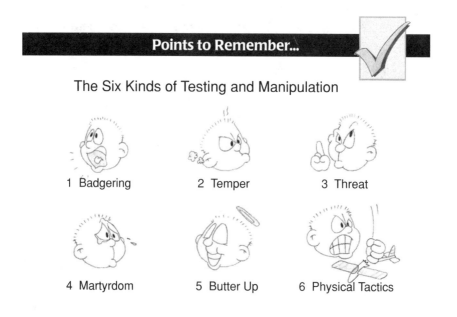

1 Badgering   2 Temper   3 Threat

4 Martyrdom   5 Butter Up   6 Physical Tactics

Questions for Christian Practice

1. Read Hebrews 12:7-11. How does God treat us as His children? What does this say about how we should parent our own children?

2. Most children are naturals at testing and manipulation. Which testing behaviors by your children deserve an Oscar Award?

3. Describe a time when you handled your child's testing behavior well. Describe a time when you gave in or got upset at your child's testing behavior.

4.Which testing behavior by your child is the most difficult for you to handle? How will you handle this behavior when you implement 1-2-3 Magic for Christian Parents?

5. Describe the concept of "delayed tester." How will you deal with your child if he exhibits this behavior?

11
Love in Action

A refusal to correct is a refusal to love; love your children by disciplining them.

Proverbs 13:24 The Message

According to the Bible, parents show love by disciplining their children. In this chapter we'll present some real-life, down-to-earth examples of parents attempting to love their children through good discipline. Our examples will show you the 1-2-3 in action and help give you a feel for counting. The stories and commentaries will also illustrate some of the basic do's and don'ts involved with the procedure. And sometimes, when the parents or teachers here don't do well with their discipline the first time around, we'll give them another chance to correct their mistakes.

Sibling Rivalry

Nine-year-old John and his seven-year-old sister Brittany are best of friends and best of enemies. They are playing with Legos on the living room floor. Dad is watching the football game on TV and so far is amazed the kids are getting along so well, but the fun is about to end.

"Brittany, I need another wheel for my tank," says John sweetly.
"No, John, I've got it on my wagon," says Brittany nervously.
(Dad squirms in his chair. It's fourth-and-goal for the good guys.)
"Lemme just use one wheel now. I'll give it back to you later,"

suggests brother.

"No, my wagon needs four wheels," replies sister.

"Your wagon looks stupid!"

"Dad, John's gonna take one of my wheels and I had them
first!"

(Dad's team had to try for a field goal and it was blocked. Dad is
not pleased.)

"Both of you, knock it off!"

"She doesn't need to hog all the wheels. There aren't enough
for me to make what I want, and they're my Legos."

"But I made this first!"

"OK, kids, that's 1 for both of you."

"She's an idiot." (John smashes his creation and leaves.)

Comment: Pretty good discipline job by Dad. Perhaps he should have
counted a little bit sooner instead of growling, "Knock it off!" Should
Dad have counted John for smashing his tank or badmouthing his sister?
Some parents would count these behaviors, but others wouldn't because
the tank was John's (and it can be rebuilt). John may also be doing the
right thing by leaving the situation.

Second chance: Let's give Dad another chance to improve his technique:

"Brittany, I need another wheel for my tank," says John sweetly.

"No, John, I've got it on my wagon," says Brittany nervously.

(Dad squirms in his chair. It's fourth-and-goal for the good guys.)

"Lemme just use one wheel now. I'll give it back to you later,"
suggests brother.

"No, my wagon needs four wheels," replies sister.

"Your wagon looks stupid!"

"Kids, that's 1 for both of you."

(Dad's team had to try for a field goal and it was blocked. Dad is
not pleased.)

"She doesn't need to hog all the wheels. There aren't enough
for me to make what I want, and they're my Legos."

"But I made this first!"

"OK, kids, that's 2."

Comment: Dad did much better this time, especially since he was extra aggravated after his team blew its scoring opportunity. Excellent self-control and an excellent job of not taking his extra frustration out on the kids.

Four-Year-Old Speeding

Rita is four-years-old and loves to go shopping at the grocery store with her Mom. The reason she loves shopping trips is because the store has little kiddie carts she can push around just like her mother does. Rita's Mom, however, does not enjoy shopping with her daughter as much as vice versa. The reason Mom does not like these shopping trips is because, sooner or later, Rita always starts running around with the cart. Last week the little girl ran into the big shopping cart of an older gentleman. Although the man was nice about it and even laughed, Mom is afraid her daughter will hurt someone.

If Mom doesn't let Rita have a cart, the girl will throw a raging fit — guaranteed — in front of everyone in the store. Mom feels her daughter is running the show.

Mom is correct. Here's how the scene goes when Mom and Rita enter the store:

"Mom! Can I push a cart?"

"I don't think so, dear. Not today. Look at the Fuzzy Bear sign!"

"Why can't I?"

"I just told you, dear. Now please don't start giving me a hard time."

"I wanna push my own one!"

"Now stop that! That's enough! Come on, we've got a lot of things to get."

"I never get to do anything!" Rita starts crying loudly.

"OK, OK! Stop that!" Mom gets a kiddie cart for Rita. Rita grabs the cart, but Mom holds the cart for a second and looks at her daughter firmly.

"Rita, look at me. You have to promise me you won't run with the cart. You might hurt someone. Do you understand me?"

"Yes."

"And you promise you won't run with the cart?"

"Yes."

"Say I promise."

"I promise."

"OK. Now let's get our stuff. I'll put some things in your cart."

Rita does just fine for six minutes. Then she starts running with her kiddie cart, giggling as she zooms along past the spaghetti sauce. Her mother pretends she doesn't notice, then she cuts the shopping trip short after getting only one-third of the things she needed. Maybe she can come back later and get the rest of what she wants by herself.

Comment: A classic example of a child intimidating a parent with the threat of public embarrassment. Mom is intimidated into a desperate attempt at little adult reasoning ("You might hurt someone") and the elicitation of futile promises.

Let's give Mom another chance to get this one right. Actually, Rita's mother has two choices: (1) counting Rita for speeding and at count 3 taking away the cart, and (2) not letting Rita have a cart in the first place.

Option 1: Counting Rita for speeding

"Mom! Can I push a cart?"

"Yes, dear. But you have to walk with it. If I count you to 3 for running, I'll take the cart away."

Rita does fine for three minutes, then starts running with the kiddie cart.

"Rita, that's 1. At 3 you lose the cart."

Comment: This approach is much better. There will probably be hell to pay if Rita hits 3, so Mom should be ready to take the little girl out to the car for a while till she finishes her tantrum. If returning to the car is necessary, no parental "I told you so" comments are allowed.

Option 2: Not letting Rita have the kiddie cart

"Mom! Can I push a cart?"

"No. Last time you ran with it."

"Why can't I?"

"That's 1."
"I wanna push my own one!"
"That's 2."

Comment: Good work, Mom!

Dog Teasing

Four-year-old Michael has the dog backed into a corner and pushed up against the wall. The dog, normally patient, is starting to snarl. Mom intervenes.

"Michael, please don't tease the dog, honey."
(Michael giggles and continues pushing the dog against the wall.)
"That's 1."
"No! I wanna pet him." (Dog snarls again.)
"That's 2."
"I WANNA PET HIM!" (Intimidation) (Continues torturing.)
"That's 3. Upstairs."
(Michael falls on floor, releasing the dog, but yelling and crying.
  Mom drags the unwilling body to the bedroom for time out.)

Comment: Couldn't have done it better. No talking while "escorting" the child to the rest period.

Bedtime Problem

It's nine o'clock in the evening. Alex is playing an electronic game on the couch in the living room. His mother enters the room:

"Alex, it's time to get ready for bed."
Entranced with his game, Alex does not respond at all.
"Alex, That's 1."

Comment: This is a trick! Should counting be used for bedtime? The answer is no, because getting ready for bed is a Start behavior—actually, a series of Start behaviors that take a while to complete. Counting is for obnoxious or difficult behavior, such as whining, arguing, teasing, fighting or tantrums, where cooperation takes only a few seconds.

Requests

Eight-year-old Tom asks his mother if he can use his Dad's electric jig saw in the basement tool room.

"I don't think so. You better wait till Daddy's home."

"Oh come on, Mom. I know how to do it."

"No, I think it's too dangerous."

"There's nothing else to do." (Badgering, Martyrdom)

"I said no. That's 1."

"THAT'S 1! THAT'S 2! THAT'S 3! THAT'S 12! THAT'S 20! THAT'S STUPID!" (Intimidation)

"That's 2."

"Didn't know you could count that high." (Intimidation)

"That's 3, take 10 and add 5 for the mouth."

"Gee, I'll need a calculator for this one."

Mom moves toward Tom to escort him if necessary, but he goes to his bedroom.

Comment: Mom did very well—one explanation and then she counted. Mom also adds five for the smart mouth, and she has the presence of mind to stay cool in spite of the insult. When her son doesn't go to the rest period right away, she also does not get caught up in a stupid argument or little-adult conversation.

Interrupting

Mom and Dad are having an important private conversation on the couch that has to do with the health of one of their parents. Seven-year-old Michelle jumps in between them.

"Hi, guys!"

"Hi, honey. Listen, Mom and Dad have to talk about something very important for a few minutes, so you go play for a little bit."

"I wanna be here with you. I promise I won't listen."

"No, dear. Come on now, you go and play."

"I don't have anything to do." (Badgering)

"Listen, young lady. We're not going to tell you again!"

"THERE'S NOTHING ELSE FOR ME TO DO!" (Intimidation)

"Do you want a spanking!?"

(Michelle starts crying.) (Martyrdom)

"OK, that's 1."

(Michelle leaves, crying.)

Comment: Pretty sloppy job by Mom and Dad. In fairness to these parents, this is a touchy situation because Michelle's entrance is very friendly and these parents don't want to tell her what they're discussing just yet. They only get around to counting after ridiculous attempts at persuasion, threatening a spanking and risking World War III for nothing. They eventually recover and count, but some damage has still been done.

Second chance: Let's take it from the top:

"Hi, guys!"

"Hi, honey. Listen, Mom and Dad have to talk about something very important for a few minutes, so you go play for a little bit."

"I wanna be here with you. I promise I won't listen."

"That's 1."

"I don't have anything to do." (Badgering)

"That's 2."

Michelle leaves, a bit teary.

Comment: Mom and Dad probably feel a little bit guilty, but they handled the situation well. You can't give the kids everything.

Talking in Class

During geography, Sally and Marci start a conversation across the aisle. Mrs. Smith stops her discussion of crops in Argentina.

"Girls, I need your attention."

The girls stop talking for thirty seconds, but then can't resist finishing what they started.

"Sally, Marci, that's 1."
(The girls stop talking.)

Comment: Crisp and to the point. Easier on the children's self-esteem than a lot of self-righteous criticism. Counting in a situation like this also does not break the flow of instruction.

Arguing

As Mom is working in the kitchen after dinner, eleven-year-old Jeff asks:

"Can I go out after dinner to play?"
"No, dear, you still have homework to do," says Mom.
"I'll do it when I come back in, right before bed."
"That's what you said last night, honey, and it didn't work. Remember?"
"Oh, please Mom. I promise!" (Badgering, Butter Up)
"Get your homework done first, and then you can go out. If you work hard, it shouldn't take more than a half-hour."
"Why can't I just go out now!? I'll DO MY STUPID HOME-WORK!" (Intimidation)
"That's 1."
"I can't wait to grow up so I can go in the army. It's got to be more fun than living in this dump." (Martyrdom)
"That's 2."
"All right, all right, all right." (Jeff goes to start his homework.)

Comment: Mom did very well here. She tried a little negotiating, but when that didn't work she didn't get caught up in a useless argument or try to explain why her house wasn't the same as the military.

Sibling Rivalry II

Sean, 9, and Tammi, 11, are getting into it while trying to play Scrabble in the living room. Dad is washing dishes in the kitchen.

"It's my turn."
"No it isn't. You lost it 'cause you took so long."

"Give me that. I was going to pick up that one!"

"You scratched me!"

"I did not, you idiot! You started it!"

"You're so dumb it isn't funny."

 Dad enters. "What's going on here?"

"She's cheating!"

"I am not, lamebrain, you're too slow!"

"Be quiet, both of you! Tell me what happened."

 General yelling and chaos follow the ill-fated inquiry.

"OK, that's 1 for both of you."

 General yelling and chaos continue.

"That's 2."

 Sean dumps the Scrabble board over, grabs a bunch of letters, and
   throws them at the piano.

"Sean, that's 3, take a rest for 10."

Comment: Dad recovered pretty well after asking the world's dumbest question. He should have started counting earlier.

Extreme Possessiveness

Haley is four years old. She has a playdate—at her own house—with
another little girl, Alyssa, whom she has just met. Unfortunately, everything Alyssa touches, Haley tries to take away from her. Alyssa is not
aggressive at all, but just stands there looking bewildered after a new toy
has been taken from her hands.

Mom sees the pattern. Alyssa picks up a small red car. Haley moves
in and grabs it. Mom says:

"Haley, that's 1. You must let Alyssa play with something."

 Haley still doesn't let go."

"Haley, that's 2."

 The little girl releases her hold and lets Alyssa have the car.

"That's very nice of you, sweetheart."

Comment: Good job. Explain, count and praise cooperation.

Conclusion

What have our tales from the trenches taught us? Kids can certainly catch you off guard, for one thing! You have to be on your toes and—to be fair to yourself and the children—you have to make reasonable and fairly rapid decisions about what is countable and what is not. Good counting takes a little bit of practice, but once you master the skill, you'll wonder how you ever got along without this sanity-saving technique.

Key Concepts...

The "magic" of the 1-2-3 procedure is not in the counting itself. The power of the method comes primarily from your ability to accomplish two goals. Your first objective is to explain—when necessary—and then keep quiet. Your second objective is to count as calmly and unemotionally as you can. Do these two things well and your children will start listening to you!

Questions for Christian Practice

1. Read Joshua 1:9 and Isaiah 41:13. According to these verses, why can someone be confident as a parent.

2. Which of the examples in this chapter did you identify with the most? Why?

3. Describe one example from your family that could be included in this chapter.

4. Describe an encounter with your children that you felt was not handled well.

5. Describe how the same situation could have been handled better using the 1-2-3 plan.

12
More Serious Offenses

A fool despises his father's instruction, but he who receives correction is prudent.

Proverbs 15:5 (NKJV)

Despite the attempts of Chrisitan parents to teach wisdom to their children, some older preteens still do some foolish things. These actions may fall into the category of Stop behavior, but they are too serious for our counting and time-out procedures. Included in this worrisome list of childhood exploits are lying, stealing, physical fights, cutting school, behavioral problems during school, bullying, property damage, pranks, not coming home, staying out late, smoking and starting fires. Stronger—but non-abusive—action is now required on a parent's part. You want to make sure your kids do not repeat these more troublesome activities, but you also don't want to exasperate your offspring.

Some normal pre-adolescent children, especially boys, engage in isolated incidents that include the unusual and harmful activities listed above. Sometimes these kids are influenced by other children to do things they wouldn't otherwise do. I Corinthians 15:3 states, "Bad company corrupts good character." Exercising temporary poor judgment, these youngsters are going along for the ride. When parents respond with a firm hand and a fair punishment, these first-time offenders do not become repeat offenders. This chapter will help you deal with such incidents.

Other times, however, the trouble-producing motivation comes from inside the child himself. When a child starts showing a pattern of unusually hostile, aggressive, rule-breaking behavior, we begin to worry—especially as the youngster gets older. That's why we are so interested in early prevention: *The older they are, the harder kids are to change.* This chapter will help you manage more upsetting childhood behavior reasonably, firmly and calmly.

Most parents will not need to use this chapter a lot—or perhaps even at all. But when it is necessary, the kind of targeted, rational management described here is essential in preventing the problem behavior of vulnerable, higher-risk children from escalating as these kids grow up.

Oppositional Defiance and Conduct Disorder

Although we do not totally understand why some children start down a destructive path of behavior, we do know a few things. Two motives that have been implicated in the more serious behavioral problems listed before are (1) hostile and vengeful inclinations and (2) thrill seeking. Hostile or vengeful impulses, for example, may drive behavior such as fighting, bullying and damaging property. Thrill seeking may be involved in smoking, cutting school and starting fires. Many problem behaviors, of course, can involve both motives. When this is the case, the reinforcement a young lad gets from engaging in a "double-motive" activity can be even more powerful and dangerous.

Adolescents and preteens who consistently engage in aggressive, destructive rule-breaking behavior that hurts others or damages property are often diagnosed with Conduct Disorder (CD). Their troublesome activities often reflect the two motives of hostile aggression and thrill seeking. These CD children also often have problems with learning disabilities, attention deficit disorder, language and communication, and the ability to read social cues. As you may have guessed, Conduct Disorder is the modern euphemism for juvenile delinquency.

Preadolescents who sometimes seem to get addicted to hostile and vengeful behavior are often referred to as Oppositional Defiant Disorder (ODD) children. While CD youths may want to hurt you, ODD kids simply like to aggravate you. ODD kids are negative, defiant and can't take no for an answer. They deliberately annoy other people, are in turn easily annoyed themselves, and blame everybody else for anything that goes wrong. ODD kids are Super Brats, and they are no fun to live with.

ODD probably has some genetic basis, but this disorder can also be caused—as well as seriously aggravated—by sloppy, inconsistent, angry and overly wordy parenting. In any case, ODD behavior starts at home. And when poor parenting is part of the picture, Oppositional Defiant kids can graduate to become Conduct Disorder kids; they simply take their troublesome behavior out of the house and into the community. CD teens are dangerous kids with treacherous futures.

One of the goals of *1-2-3 Magic for Christian Parents* is to prevent oppositional defiance from starting in the first place by means of reasonable, gentle and solid biblical parenting. A second goal of *1-2-3 Magic for Christian Parents* is to eliminate early ODD behavior problems—once they have started—so they don't change into Conduct Disorder. Get rid of early ODD and you cut the risk of later trouble tremendously.

For most parents, who don't have kids who are at risk for major Oppositional Defiant problems, the basic *1-2-3 Magic* program will probably be sufficient. With higher-risk children who engage in more serious problem behavior, parents will need to pay attention to what we call the Major/Minor System.

> **Quik Tip...**
>
> One goal of 1-2-3 Magic is to prevent Oppositional Defiant Disorder (ODD) through firm and reasonable parenting. Where ODD already exists, another goal of our program is to get rid of it, so ODD doesn't change later into Conduct Disorder—the modern term for juvenile delinquency.

The Major/Minor System

Your next door neighbor rings your front door bell on a beautiful summer day. This fellow has never been the most pleasant person in the world, but today he is furious. He informs you that your nine-year-old son, Doug, just put a rock through his garage window. Deliberately. Your neighbor wants to know what you're going to do about it and how you're going to punish the kid.

You are shocked, embarrassed and incredulous. You apologize to the aggravated man and tell him you'll certainly take care of it. Doug isn't a nasty problem child, but you know he's had a few run-ins with this guy, who does tend to be a real grouch sometimes. If your boy did throw a rock through the neighbor's garage window, that would obviously be Stop behavior, but it wouldn't make much sense to run to the back door and say, "Doug, that's 1." "That's 3, take 5 and add 15 for the seriousness of the offense" would also seem too mild. Some punishment may be called for, but even then, you still want to avoid a lot of the excess talking and emotion that will only make things worse.

Fortunately, there is a very simple punishment system that you can set up to handle serious problems like this with a minimum of upset and confusion. It's called the Major/Minor System. With the Major/Minor System you will establish appropriate Major or Minor punishments/ consequences for corresponding Major or Minor offenses. The Major/Minor System is applied differently depending upon how much trouble you've had in the past with your child. Is this the first time that you've had a serious problem with this child, or have there been repeated episodes?

The Major/Minor System for First-Time Offenses

With first time offenses, like Doug in our example above, you only need to deal with the problem at hand. You do not need to make a big list of behavior and punishments like you may do with repeated problems.

So let's imagine that after your irate neighbor leaves, you track down Doug. You tell him about your conversation with Mr. Antagonisky from next door. Then you ask your son what happened. You remain calm and "put on your active listening shoes" (see Chapter 25). Doug is not a bad kid, and you're determined to hear him out first, then determine what needs to be done.

Doug tells you that he was playing catch in the backyard with his friend, Chris. They were using a tennis ball. At one point Doug missed Chris' throw and it went into Antagonisky's yard, where Mr. A. was tending his flowers. Doug retrieved the ball, but while doing so, he accidentally stepped on one of Mr. A.'s stupid plants. Doug said that the guy then went ballistic, screaming and swearing at both boys and also looking physically threatening. In frustration as well as anger—and also not wanting to look scared—Doug had turned around and thrown the ball in the general direction of the neighbor's garage. He wasn't aiming at the small window, he said, but he did hear the sound of shattering glass.

How should you apply the Major/Minor System? Tell your son that even though Mr. A. is not the most diplomatic person in the world, Doug exercised poor judgment during the incident by letting his own temper get the best of him and throwing the ball at the garage. Doug therefore is going to have to accept several consequences, and the consequences here will not involve time out. First, the boy will go back and tell Antagonisky that he, Doug, will clean up the glass in the garage and pay for a replacement pane and the installation costs. Doug will also ask Mr. A. if he would like the plant replaced, and pay for that if necessary. You tell Doug that he can apologize if he so desires, but even if he doesn't, he must be polite and civil during the conversation—even if Antagonisky is not.

This punishment constitutes a major consequence for your son. Your assignment will be no small chore for the young lad. Doug does as instructed, though, and the problem is resolved. You tell your boy you're proud of him and the way he handled the situation. No other consequences—or lectures—are necessary.

By the way, you, the parent here, also did a good job. You did not beat down your son because you were embarrassed, nor did you let your boy off the hook because of your dislike for your next door neighbor.

The Major/Minor System for Repeat Offenses

What if, on the other hand, you've had a number of more serious problems with your ten-year-old son, Mike? In the last several months, Mike's been late to school three times (you think on purpose) and come home in the evening more than an hour late twice. You think he smells like he's been smoking a few times, he's been carrying matches, and you're never sure if he's lying about doing his homework. Mike's grades have slipped from a B+ to a C+ average in the last two quarters, and you really don't care for one of his new friends. Your son also seems less communicative.

When kids start acting up like this, it's easy to get so irritated so often that all you can think of is doling out punishment. When a child does something right, you ignore the good deed and think, "Well, it's about time!" When he does something wrong, however, you angrily jump all over him.

This approach cleary violates scripture. "Fathers, do not exasperate your children..." (Ephesians 6:4). This defensive and aggressive stance your part also runs the risk of making the child so angry that he is

Quik Tip...

Remember that—even with more serious offenses—fits of temper and righteous indignation from you can ruin the effectiveness of whatever punishments or consequences are chosen. You need to be decisive and calm.

more likely to engage in vengeful and hostile—as well as perhaps thrill-seeking—behavior, and the reaction and counterreaction sequence can be the start of a domestic war, with the result that your child's future is in great jeopardy. Instead of that unproductive, knee-jerk type of parenting, your strategy with Mike should involve two primary lines of attack: (1) improving your relationship with your boy through regular doses of praise, one-on-one shared fun, affection and active listening and (2) setting up the Major/Minor System.

We'll discuss how to improve a relationship with a child more specifically in Part V. Here we'll focus on the Major/Minor System. You will also set up a well-defined system of behavioral consequences for Mike. The consequences or punishments will depend on the seriousness of the behavior involved, varying from major offenses to minor transgressions (minor offenses here are still more serious than countable problems). Actually, it's usually helpful to have a three-level, Major/Medium/Minor list of consequences that include variations of groundings, fines, chores, community service or educational activities. For example:

Major Consequences

Grounding: two weeks restriction to room after dinner and on weekends; no electronic entertainment (TV, computer, games) or phone

Fine: $25 or pay back double the value of stolen or damaged articles

Chores: 15 hours work around the house

Community service: 15 hours volunteer work at church or other institution

Educational activity: research subject (e.g., smoking) and write quality eight-page paper, attend group counseling

Medium Consequences

Grounding: one-week restriction to room after dinner and on-weekends; no electronic entertainment (TV, computer, games) or phone

Fine: $10 or pay back double the value of stolen or damaged articles

Chores: eight hours work around the house

Community service: eight hours volunteer work at church or other institution

Educational activity: research subject (e.g., smoking) and write quality four-page paper

Minor Consequences

Grounding: two day restriction to room after dinner; no electronic entertainment (TV, computer, games) or phone

Fine: $5 or pay back double the value of stolen or damaged articles

Chores: four hours work around the house

Community service: four hours volunteer work at church or other institution

Educational activity: research subject (e.g., smoking) and write quality two-page paper

The punishments for Major offenses are greater than the punishments for Medium ones, and Medium consequences are bigger than those for Minor problems. The above ideas are only suggestions: These guidelines will certainly be altered by individual families. (Over the years we have learned that *there will always be* some people who think we are too strict, and others who think we are not strict enough!) Keep in mind that even the Minor offenses described in this chapter are still more serious than countable things such as arguing, yelling, teasing, whining and so on.

Once you have come up with your punishment classifications, you decide which behavior merits which class of punishment. When that misbehavior occurs, one of the consequences from the list is implemented (not the whole list!). This process saves a lot of effort and deliberation, and also lets your youngster know the consequences beforehand if he decides to mess up. Some parents even let the child choose the consequence — once the Major, Medium or Minor category has been chosen.

Recall that your son Mike was acting up more in the last few months. With Mike you work out the following classifications:

Major Offenses

Coming home more than two hours late

Playing with or starting any fire without parent present

Medium Offenses

Coming home one to two hours late

Getting to school more than five minutes late

Lying about more serious matters

Carrying matches or lighter

Minor Offenses

Coming home up to one hour late

Getting to school less than five minutes late

Lying about homework

Once the system is set up, when Mike pulls a fast one, you simply categorize it and determine the consequence. No yelling or screaming by you is allowed, of course, though a *short* explanation or discussion may occasionally be in order (see Chapter 20). What if the youngster does something that you didn't put on the original Major/Minor list? You just classify it as Major, Medium or Minor and then pick a punishment.

You can adjust the Major/Minor System after you set it up, but be careful not to make punishments so harsh that they backfire. One family, I remember, had a Major/Minor System in place, like the one described above, for their twelve-year-old son. Then one day they found out that the boy had stolen a bike. The major punishments suddenly didn't seem like strong enough consequences for this act, so they told the boy he was grounded for a year! A discipline response like this will never work because it will be impossible to enforce and it will probably start a war. A better punishment would have been a grounding for a month and a requirement to pay back the value of the bike.

If you've been having a serious problem with repeated offenses, you can also make a chart that keeps track of the number of days in a row in which the child stays free of trouble. There might even be a reward for this good performance, such as a special outing with one parent (not with the whole family!). If serious problems continue in spite of the Major/Minor System—and in spite of your working to improve the relationship with the youngster—it is time for an evaluation with a professional.

Several other prevention-oriented thoughts are in order here. If you have a young lad who seems inclined along ODD/CD lines, research has shown that there are a number of important factors that can help prevent future problems. And these factors are—at least to some extent—under parental control. These problem-reducing forces include discipline consistency day-to-day, discipline consistency between parents, marital stability, parental mental health and close—but reasonable—supervision of the child.

> **Quik Tip...**
> When using the Major/Minor System, make sure the consequences aren't so harsh that they backfire. And build in some kind of reward for a child's going a number of days or weeks without any problem at all. That's an accomplishment that should be recognized!

Lying

The problem of children lying is included in this chapter for two reasons: (1) lying itself is a more serious offense and (2) lying is often used to cover up other more serious offenses. Lying drives some parents crazy, and managing this problem is often confusing and difficult. Therefore we'll try to provide some basic guidelines.

There are basically two kinds of lies. The first kind involves making up stories that are designed to impress other people and build up one's ego. This type of verbal fabrication is not common in children. The second—and by far the most common type—is lying to avoid trouble.

This type may involve covering up a past misdeed or trying to get out of some unpleasant task. Kids who steal, for example, will almost always lie about the theft when they are initially confronted. Other kids lie about not having homework so they won't have to face a boring job.

Many parents get so upset about lying that they act as though the world were coming to an end. The Bible does clearly state that lying is wrong. "Do not lie to each other. Since you have taken off your old self with its practices" (Colossians 3:9). But this does not elevate dishonesty into something worse than all the other negative behaviors that parents must address. It is just another area where Christian parents must train their children in righteousness.

What Should You Do About Lying?

The school calls on Tuesday at 1:00 to tell you that your ten-year-old son, Tom, got into a fight with a boy named Davey Smith at lunchtime. At 3:45 Tom comes home. Mom starts the conversation like this:

> "How was your day?"
> "Good. You made me my favorite sandwich for lunch."
> "Speaking of lunchtime, how did that go?"
> "Fine, we played some baseball."
> "Anything unusual happen?
> "No."
> "OK, listen, young man. You're lying to me. I got a call from
>   the school today and Mr. Pasquini told me you got into a fight
>   with Davey Smith...etc., etc."

In this conversation the parent is "cornering" the youngster. Sure, this parent wants to get some information from her son, but *first* Mom wants to *test* the boy to see if he'll tell the truth. Is this the right way to handle the situation? The answer is no.

When you know some kind of trouble has occurred, a primary rule is this: Don't corner children. Imagine that one night right after dinner you give your child the third degree about whether or not he has homework. He denies having any homework six times and then finally, after your seventh question, he breaks down and admits that he has some arithmetic to do. By this time, of course, you are furious, but you also feel victorious that you finally got the truth out of the kid.

But what has really just happened? You have given your child six times to practice lying! You may think to yourself, "Sooner or later he'll realize he can't fool me and he'll give up." Sometimes kids will give up, but many children will continue trying to take the easy way out first. They will simply work to become better liars and you will be helping to provide them with their practice sessions.

Here's a more constructive approach. Imagine something bad has happened. You either know the truth or you don't. If you don't know what occurred, ask the youngster once what happened. If he tells you the story and you find out later that the child lied, punish him for whatever the offense was as well as for the lie, using the Major/Minor System.

Try not to surprise the child by asking your question "impulsively," or on the spur of the moment. Many kids simply respond impulsively. They lie, but their real desire is just to end the conversation, get rid of you and stay out of trouble.

What if something bad has happened and you already know all the gory details? You might say something like this: "I want you to tell me the story of what happened at lunch today, but not right now. Think about it a while and we'll talk in fifteen minutes. But remember I already talked with Mr. Pasquini." No lectures or tantrums from you.

There is another option many parents use when (1) they already know what happened and (2) the child is very likely to lie about the event no matter how the questions are phrased. In this case you simply tell the youngster what you know and then calmly mete out the punishment. You do not even give the child the chance to lie. Under these circumstances many kids will blow up and accuse you of not trusting them (Testing Tactic #2, temper). Manage the testing by ignoring their statement or counting them, and end the conversation with, "I'm sure you'll do better next time."

When you have a child who uses lying regularly to avoid unpleasant tasks, such as chores or homework, try to fix the problem—as much as you can—so that lying does not seem necessary to the child. If your son continually lies about homework, for example, work out some kind of communication with the teacher, such as a daily assignment sheet. Then use the tactics described in Chapter 17, such as the PNP routine and Rough Checkout. For chores, consider fixing the problem by the judicious use of other Start behavior strategies (see Chapter 13).

Lying doesn't mean that your kids don't love you or that they are bound to grow up to become inmates in a federal penitentiary. Lying is a problem, though, and it needs to be managed carefully and thoughtfully. You should strive to teach honesty to your children. "Each of you must put off falsehood and speak truthfully to his neighbor" (Ephesians 4:25). But be careful, because over the years frequent emotional overreactions from you—combined with badgering and cornering—can help produce an Accomplished Liar.

Congratulations! You have just learned parenting Step 1: Controlling Obnoxious Behavior. You are ready to begin counting and you are prepared for testing and manipulation from your kids. So now we're on to the next giant parenting step: Encouraging Good Behavior.

Points to Remember...

1. A principal goal of the Major/Minor System is the prevention of bigger behavior problems later on.

2. Many parents won't ever need to use this part of the program.

3. Use the Major/Minor for more serious problems, such as stealing, bullying, property damage, hours violations and lying.

4. When implementing consequences, be decisive and—although it's very hard—be as calm and reasonable as you can!

Questions for Christian Practice

1. Read Galatians 6:7-8 and I Samuel 26:23. How does God respond to our good and bad behavior? How can this be applied to parenting?

2. List some positive things your child has done lately? How will you praise him for these positive behaviors?

3. Imagine a more serious misbehavior by your child that would go beyond the 1-2-3 approach. Now brainstorm a plan for handling this situation.

4. Develop your game plan for addressing the problem of lying.

5. If you do need the Major/Minor System, list some of the possible Major, Medium and Minor consequences you could use. (You may consider letting your child help you develop your final list.)

Part IV

Encouraging
Good Behavior

13

7 Start-Behavior Tactics

Train up a child in the way he should go, and when he is old he will not turn from it.

Proverbs 22:6

The Bible encourages parents to train their children. The result of this training, according to Proverbs 22:6, is that children will not turn from it. In other words, our training today pays off in the future. The training we provide for our children today becomes the character they take into adulthood. So we now turn our attention to the second big parenting job: encouraging your children to do the positive things you want them to do. We call this behavior category Start behavior, because you want your children to start doing their schoolwork, going to bed, eating their supper, cleaning their rooms and getting up and out in the morning. Training your children to do these things will have benefits far beyond the immediate accomplishment of these tasks.

Recall that Start behavior requires more motivation from children than Stop behavior. While it may only take one second to stop whining or arguing, tasks such as doing homework or getting up and off to school may require thirty minutes or more. Kids not only have to start these jobs, they also have to continue and finish them. Counting difficult behavior is fairly easy. When it comes to positive behavior, however, moms and dads have to be more skilled motivators.

It's a good idea, when beginning this program, to use counting first for a week to ten days before tackling Start behavior. If you try to do the whole program at once (both Stop and Start problems), it may be a little too much to keep straight. Equally important, it will also be considerably easier to get the kids to do the good things if you have first gotten back in control of the house by effectively managing their obnoxious conduct.

When you begin using your Start behavior tactics, don't be surprised if you run into testing and manipulation. Remember, your daughter is not going to thank you for encouraging her to clean her room. If you have worked on counting negative behavior first, you will have had a fair amount of experience in dealing with Stop behavior, such as testing, before you tackle the task of getting the kids to do the good things. So have the 1-2-3 ready in your back pocket; you can pull that tool out whenever necessary.

Key Concepts...

With Start behavior, you can use more than one tactic at a time for a particular problem. You may even come up with some of your own strategies. Remember: Train the kids to do what you want, or keep quiet!

There are seven Start behavior tactics you can consider using. Sometimes you may use just one tactic, but other times you may use two or three for the same problem. While counting obnoxious behavior is fairly straightforward, you can be more creative and flexible when managing positive behavior. In fact, many parents and teachers have come up with useful and imaginative ideas that are not on our list.

Here are our seven strategies for encouraging good behavior:

1. Positive reinforcement
2. Simple requests
3. Kitchen timers
4. The Docking System
5. Natural consequences
6. Charting
7. Counting (different version)

When dealing with Start behavior, keep in mind one of the basic rules of *1-2-3 Magic*: *Train the children or keep quiet!* In the 1-2-3 program there is a method for handling just about every kind of problem your kids can throw at you. So use these methods! Kids, for example, are not born to be natural room cleaners. If the child isn't cleaning his room, train him to clean it. Otherwise, be quiet, clean it yourself or close the door and don't look. Training, however, does not mean nagging, arguing, yelling or hitting.

With these rules in mind, let's take a look at the seven tactics you will use to get the kids to do what they're supposed to.

1. Positive Reinforcement

Angry people make noise; happy people remain silent. We all suffer from a biological curse that motivates us to say something to our kids when we're angry at them, but to keep quiet when the little ones are doing what we want them to do. Imagine it's a Sunday in October and I'm watching a football game in the afternoon. My two children are in the next room playing a game with each other, having a great time and getting along very well. What do you think the chances are that I'm going to get up out of my chair, walk all the way into the next room, and say, "Gee, I'm delighted you guys are having such a good time!"? That would be a great thing, but the chances of my doing it are about zero. Why? Because when adults are happy and content themselves, they are not particularly motivated to do anything more than what they're already doing.

But imagine that my children in the next room start fighting and screaming. Why do they behave this way?! I can't even hear the football game!! Now I am motivated—I'm mad. Now the chances of my getting up, running into the other room and yelling at the kids to keep quiet are high. Anger is a much better motivator than contentment. The result is that our kids are more likely to hear from us when we have negative rather than positive feedback. Youngsters as well as spouses can start feeling they're just a pain in the neck to us.

One powerful antidote to this unfortunate biological orientation inside us is praise or positive verbal reinforcement. "A word aptly spoken is like apples of gold in settings of silver" (Proverbs 25:11). The idea in the verse is that the right words (praise) said at the right time (often) can produce tremendous results. Your praise and other positive interactions with your kids should outnumber your negative comments by a ratio of about three or four to one. If you look, you shouldn't have trouble finding something to reinforce:

"Thanks for doing the dishes."

"You started your homework all by yourself!"

"That dog really likes you."

"You kids did a good job of getting along during the movie."

"I think you got ready for school in record time this morning!"

"Good job on that math test, John."

"I saw you out on the soccer field. You played hard—good hustle!"

"That's wonderful! I can't believe it! How on earth did you do that?!"

Once you've gotten the kids successfully carrying out a particular Start behavior, positive reinforcement can help keep the cooperation or good performance going. Many parents, for example, praise or thank their kids for complying with simple requests or for following a bedtime or homework routine.

Quik Tip...
Praise in front of other people and unexpected praise are potent reinforcers. These tactics will make your children feel very proud. They'll really appreciate you for your thoughtfulness—and they'll keep up the good work!

Keep a sensitive eye on your son or daughter, though, because praise should be tailored to some extent to each child. Some kids like rather elaborate, syrupy and emotional verbal reinforcement, while others do not. Your eight-year-old daughter, for instance, gets 100 percent on Wednesday on her spelling pretest. You say, "Oh Melissa, that's just marvelous! I can't believe it! We're going to frame this paper and also fax it to grandma in Florida!!" Melissa eats it up. Melissa's eleven-year-old brother, however, would be nauseated by that kind of talk. For him, "Good job—keep up the good work," and a pat on the shoulder might be enough. Your job is to praise the child, not to embarrass him.

There are two additional devices you can use to make praise a more effective boost to a child's self-esteem: (1) *praise in front of other people* and (2) *unexpected praise*. "Do not let any unwholesome talk come out of your mouths, but only what is helpful for building others up according to their needs, that it may benefit those who listen" (Ephesians 4:29). Building your kids up in front of others as well as unexpectedly will definitely benefit them. While you're talking to your next door neighbor, for example, your daughter Kelsey walks up. You interrupt your conversation and say, "You should have seen Kelsey out there on the soccer field today. Those other kids never knew what hit them!" Kelsey will beam with pride.

Unexpected praise can also be quite memorable for a child. Your son is upstairs doing his homework. You call from the bottom of the stairs, "Hey, Jordan!" Jordan has no idea what's coming next. You then say, "Did I tell you what a great job you did on the yard?" Jordan will be pleased — and perhaps a little relieved!

How do you keep offering praise and encouragement on a regular basis? As mentioned before, this task is surprisingly difficult, since most of us tend to shut up when we are content. Here are two suggestions. First, see if you can make two or three positive comments for every one negative comment (by the way, one count is one negative comment). These positive remarks don't have to be made at the same time, of course. They can be made later. If the two-or-three-to-one ratio idea doesn't appeal to you, a second strategy is to have a quota system. Each day you make a deal with yourself that you will make at least five positive comments to each child (consider doing the same with your spouse).

2. Simple Requests

The problem with simple requests is that they are not so simple. Parental requests to children can be made more or less effective by the parent's tone of voice, the spontaneity of the request and the phrasing of the demand.

We all have different voices. When she was younger, my daughter had several different variations of the simple expression, "Dad!" One "Dad!" meant I'm excited and want to show you something. Another "Dad!" meant I want assistance because my brother is teasing me. And yet a third "Dad!" (during her teen years) meant, "Cool it, oldtimer, you're embarrassing me in public!"

Parents have different voices too; the voice we're concerned about here is called "chorevoice." Chorevoice has a quality of "You're not doing what I expect and it's really irritating and what's the matter with you and when are you going to learn..." etc., etc. Chorevoice has an aggravated, nagging and anxious tone that most children themselves find aggravating. When this parental tone of voice is coupled with a request, therefore, it makes cooperation less likely because you are now asking an angry child to cooperate.

A good antidote to chorevoice is a businesslike, matter-of-fact presentation. "John, it is now time to start your homework" or "Taylor, bedtime." This tone of voice implies, "You may not like this but it's got to be done now." Testing is much less likely when requests are made in a matter-of-fact way. And—believe it or not—the mere tone of voice can also say, "If you push me or test me, you'll get counted."

The *spontaneity* of a parental request can also be a cooperation killer. Your son is outside playing baseball with some friends. You go to the front door and ask him if he'd come in and take out the garbage. He blows his stack and you think, "What is the big deal?" You are correct that your boy overreacted, but the big deal was not the garbage. The big deal to him was the spontaneity. What do you expect the youngster to say, "Thanks for offering me this opportunity to be of service to the family"?

No one likes spur-of-the-moment interruptions that involve unpleasant tasks. You don't like them either, but you are often stuck with such intrusions. But we're not talking about getting *you* to cooperate here, we're talking about getting *your kids* to cooperate. And we're also not saying your children shouldn't have chores to do. They should help out around the house. The point is this: Try to structure these tasks so that spontaneous requests are seldom necessary.

Finally, the phrasing of a request can also make a difference in how kids respond. Phrasing a request as a question and adding the ridiculous "we" to the statement will often insure noncompliance or testing and manipulation. A super-sweet "Don't we think it's about time to start our homework?" for example, is almost guaranteed to elicit a negative response. "I want your schoolwork complete by five o'clock" is better.

What if, in spite of everything, your simple request still does no good? We'll come back to that question after we've discussed several other Start behavior options.

3. Kitchen Timers

Kitchen timers are wonderful devices for encouraging good behavior in children. The ones I think are most useful are the sixty-minute, wind-up variety, though many other kinds exist. The people who manufacture timers think they're for baking cakes. They're not—timers are for raising kids! Kitchen timers can be a great help for just about any Start behavior, whether it's picking up, feeding the fish, getting up in the morning, taking the garbage out or going to bed. Kids, especially the younger ones, have a natural tendency to want to beat a ticking mechanical device. The problem then becomes a case of man against machine (rather than child against parent).

These portable motivational gadgets can also be used, if you like, to time the time outs themselves. Many kids actually prefer doing the time out with a timer. You can also take timers in the car with you and use them—as we'll see later—to help control sibling rivalry. Timers can be part of routines for bedtime or bath time or getting up and out in the morning.

Timers also can sometimes soften the blow of unavoidable spontaneous requests. A friend of yours calls and says she'll be over in fifteen minutes. You say to your five-year-old daughter, "You've got three things in the kitchen I would like picked up and put in your room. I'm setting the timer for ten minutes and I'll bet you can't beat it!"

Her response will often be, "Oh yes I can!" and the youngster will be hurrying off to do the job. You could take this same approach to get an eleven-year-old to pick up, but you would phrase your request in a more matter-of-fact manner. If the child doesn't respond before the timer dings, you can use the Docking System or a version of natural consequences (see below).

Kitchen timers are also effective because they are not testable. Machines cannot be emotionally manipulated. Imagine you had to remind your son to call his grandmother to thank her for the birthday present she mailed. Your son balks, so you set the timer for ten minutes. The boy's response is "This is stupid!" (Testing Tactic # 2, temper). Your response is silence. The timer's response is tick, tick, tick.

4. The Docking System

The principle of docking wages is this: If you don't do the work, you don't get paid. The basic idea of the Docking System is similar: If you don't do the work, I'll do it for you and you'll pay me. The Docking System is for children who are kindergarten age or above.

This plan, of course, requires that the kids first have a source of funds from an allowance, work around the house, birthday gifts or some other financial reservoir. You can consider starting an allowance with children who are about five years old or more. The payment doesn't have to be anything large, but it's a good idea to have half of it based on completing jobs around the house (e.g., cleaning the bedroom, chores, homework). The other half is simply given to the child because he is part of the family—and also so you are sure you have some leverage when it comes time to use the Docking procedure.

Let's imagine you've been having discussions with your nine-year-old son about getting a dog. The child wants the dog, but you wisely object that you're concerned he won't feed it properly. Let's assume you get the dog (partly because you want one, too).

Quik Tip...

With the Docking System, you tell the kids, "I have good news and bad news. The good news is that if you forget a chore, I'll do it for you. The bad news is that you're going to pay me for helping you out." Then tell them the exact amount involved.

You then tell the child what the deal will be. He's nine and gets about $3 per week allowance. You want the dog fed after 6:00 each night. If he feeds the dog then, fine. If he doesn't get to feeding the dog soon after 6:00, you have good news and bad news. The good news is that you will feed the dog for the boy. The bad news is that you charge to feed other people's dogs, and for this mutt it will be 15 cents per feeding taken off your son's $3 allowance. The child readily agrees, since he's so happy about getting the dog to begin with.

Here's how events might play out. The first night you're in the kitchen making dinner, it's 6:10, there's no one around, and the dog's hungry. You wait. At quarter after your son comes running in asking if you fed the dog. You say, "No." He says, "Good!" and he feeds the dog. You praise the boy, "Hey, great job! That dog was sure happy to see you."

The second night you're in the kitchen and it's 6:20. The dog is looking hungry, but you wait. Now it's 6:30 and the dog is licking your legs! So you finally feed the hungry animal. At 6:40 your boy comes running in:

"Did you feed the dog?"
"Yes, I did. I charged you 15 cents from your allowance."
"WELL WHAT DID YOU DO THAT FOR?!" (Yelling)
"That's 1."

This is not a discussion. It *was* a discussion, but now it's an attack. It's simply one version of testing tactic # 2, temper, and it should be counted. You discuss discussions and you count attacks. In this kind of situation, it's extremely difficult to resist the temptation to get into angry, little-adult types of comments, such as, "Do you remember when we bought this stupid animal for you? What did you say? You said, 'I'll feed the dog every single night. No problem!' Right! Well, here we are on only the second night and I'm already feeding your dog! I'm sick of doing everything around here for all you people!"

What you're saying may be absolutely correct, but tirades like this will do no good. Parental tantrums and righteous indignation will, in fact, cause harm. Your tirade will do two things. First, the outburst will damage your relationship with your child. Second, your blow-up will ruin the effect of the money the boy was docked. So be quiet and let the money do the talking. If money doesn't seem to have much clout with this particular lad, take minutes off TV, game or computer time or use some other reasonable consequence.

The Docking System is good for lots of things. How many times have you had the feeling that parenting is unfair? About nine million times? This unfairness applies especially to the moms, who often feel they get stuck with all the extra chores around the house. Well, think of this: Now, if you are going to have to do all that stuff, you're going to get paid for it!

Have you ever said to your kids, for example, "I'm happy to do your laundry on Saturday. All you have to do is get your clothes down to the washer by 9:00. But I'll be darned if I'm going to go up to your room every weekend to get your dirty underwear out from underneath your bed!"

Now let's imagine you're going to use the Docking System for laundry. You say this: "I'm happy to do your laundry on Saturday mornings. All you have to do is get your clothes down to the washer by 9:00. If you don't get your clothes down by 9:00, I will go up to your room to get your dirty things. But I charge for that service. And for a pile the size of the one you usually have, it will probably cost you seventy-five cents to a dollar."

5. Natural Consequences

In chapter five we covered the principle of sowing and reaping found in Galatians 6:7-8. The idea is that children often need consequences in order for them to change. When using the counting procedure, the parent provides the consequences. With natural consequences, however, you let the big, bad world teach the child what works and what doesn't. There are times when your staying out of some problems is the best approach.

Suppose you have a fourth grader who is taking piano lessons for the first time. She is not practicing as she should, however, and can't sleep at night because she's worrying that her piano teacher will be mad.

What should you do? Nothing right away. See if the natural consequence of not practicing (teacher's displeasure) will alter your daughter's behavior. Some piano teachers are very good at getting uncooperative kids to tickle the ivories on a regular basis. If after a few weeks the teacher's efforts don't work, try other Start behavior tactics, such as using the timer or charting. But leave the situation alone in the beginning.

Or, suppose you have a boy in the sixth grade. Because you're in a hurry every morning, this young fellow is supposed to make his own lunch, with goods that you buy, and then brown bag it to school. It seems like every other day, though, he is telling you how hungry he was at lunch with nothing to eat. What should you do? Relax, don't lecture, and leave the responsibility squarely on his shoulders. Let the natural consequence (his empty stomach) talk to him instead of his mother talking to him. Give him some encouragement by saying something like this: "I'm sure you'll do better tomorrow."

Another example of a good time to use natural consequences? The wintertime dress of preteens and adolescents. All parents know that junior high and high school students think there are federal laws against zipping or buttoning up their coats in the winter. These kids do not want to appear as though their mothers dressed them in the morning. The solution? Let the cold talk to the kids if they're not dressed properly, and avoid starting the day with the obvious, aggravating comment, "You're not going out like that again, are you?!"

One final, real-life example of natural consequences. One mother I used to see years ago had a four-and-one-half-year-old boy who was driving her nuts in the morning. The boy was in preschool, but he wouldn't get dressed on time for his car pool ride. Every morning when the horn honked in the driveway, this little guy was sitting in his pajamas watching cartoons on TV. The poor Mom was tearing her hair out.

One morning this mother decided she'd had enough. The boy was in his pajamas watching cartoons when the car in the drive honked. Mom then calmly proceeded to send her son off to school in his pajamas (this was not my idea!). This youngster spent two and one half hours, with his peers, with little flowered booties on and with butterflies all over his chest. At our next session a relieved Mom reported to me that, since that day, she had never again had a problem with her son being ready for his ride.

6. Charting

Charting is a very friendly motivational technique. With charting you use something like a calendar to keep track of how well a child is doing with different Start behaviors. You can put the chart on the refrigerator door, if public acclaim is desired, or on the back of the child's bedroom door, if privacy is desired. The days of the week usually go across the top of the chart, and down the left side is a list of the tasks the child is working on, such as picking up after herself, getting to bed and clearing the table after supper. If the child completes the task to your satisfaction, you indicate this on the chart with stickers for the little kids (approximate ages four to nine) and grades or points (A-F, 5-1) for the older children.

Here's what a chart might look like. This child is working on cleaning her room, brushing her teeth and feeding her parakeet:

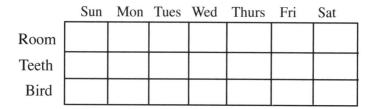

	Sun	Mon	Tues	Wed	Thurs	Fri	Sat
Room							
Teeth							
Bird							

With charting, positive reinforcement comes, we hope, from three things: the chart itself, parental praise and the inherent satisfaction of doing a good job. We call these three things *natural* reinforcers. When my daughter was nine, she decided she wanted to take piano lessons. Although this was her choice, she didn't practice regularly and—like the fourth-grader we mentioned earlier—she would worry a lot the night before her lesson that her teacher was going to be upset with her the next day when she couldn't perform well.

We first tried natural consequences, suggesting to our little girl that she work out the problem with her teacher. This tactic failed. So we next tried charting with only natural reinforcers. Our agreement was this: Each day after practicing, our daughter was to find her mother or father and tell that parent exactly how many minutes she had practiced. One of us would then write that number for that day on the chart and praise our budding concert pianist for her work. That was it. The plan worked like a charm.

> **CAUTION**
> Natural reinforcers, such as praise, sometimes aren't enough to motivate children to complete a task—especially if the kids hate the job! In these cases artificial rewards can be used; you'll try to borrow some motivation from somewhere else. It works!

Unfortunately for us parents, natural reinforcers are frequently insufficient to motivate a child to complete a particular task. Your son, for example, may simply be a natural slob—a clean room means nothing to him. Or your little girl may be attention deficit and learning disabled, and homework provides no satisfaction—but much frustration—for her.

In these cases you must use what we call *artificial* reinforcers. Artificial reinforcers mean that the child is going to earn something—which may have nothing directly to do with the task—for successful completion of that task. Since the activity doesn't provide any incentive to the child—and, in fact, may provide a negative incentive—we are going to try to borrow motivation from somewhere else. Our little girl who hates homework, for example, might earn part of her allowance, a special meal or a special time with you.

For smaller children the best ideas are often relatively small things that can be dished out frequently and in little pieces. With older kids, larger rewards that take longer to earn become more feasible. Let yourself be creative in coming up with reinforcers. Rewards certainly do not always have to be material. Some kids, for example, will work hard to earn minutes to stay up later at night, or to be able to do some special activity with one of their parents.

Here is a list of possible artificial reinforcers:

A trip for ice cream	Cash
Brightly colored tokens	Staying up past bedtime
A small toy	Renting a special movie
Renting a special game	A grab-bag surprise
Outing with a parent	Comic book or magazine
Shopping trip	Friend over for supper
Sleepover	Choice of three reinforcers
Playing a game with parent	Reading a story with parent
A "No Chore" voucher	Sleeping with dog or cat
Camping out in backyard	Special phone call
Card for a collection	Other items for collections
Snack of choice	Helping make and eat cookies
Breakfast in bed	Using power tool with supervision

Keep any chart simple. Three or four things to work on at one time is enough; more than that gets too confusing. I saw a family once who created a chart for their son on which they were attempting to rate thirty-three different behaviors every day! I had to give them an "A" for effort, but also a high rating for confusion.

Keep in mind that you probably will not want to do charting for long periods of time. Charting can become a semi-obnoxious behavioral accounting task, and the positive effects can fade when mom and dad are getting tired of filling the chart out every day. So build in "discontinuation criteria"—rules for determining when the chart is no longer necessary. You might say, for example, that if the child gets good scores (define this precisely) for two weeks running on a particular behavior, that item will be taken off the chart. When the child has earned his way off the chart entirely, it's time to go out for pizza and a movie to celebrate. If after a while the child gets worse again, you can reinstate the chart.

7. Counting for Brief Start Behavior

As mentioned earlier, one of the most frequent mistakes parents make with the 1-2-3 is attempting to use counting to get a child to do Start behavior like homework, chores or getting up and out in the morning. Recall that these tasks can take twenty minutes or more, while counting itself only produces several seconds worth of motivation.

What if the Start behavior itself, however, only required a few seconds worth of cooperation? You want your daughter to hang up her coat, feed the cat or come into the room. Counting, which is so useful for Stop behavior, can be used for some Start behavior, but only on one condition: *What you want the child to do cannot take more than about two minutes.* Your child throws her coat on the floor after school, and you ask her to pick it up. She doesn't, and you say, "That's 1." If she still refuses to comply and gets timed out, she goes and serves the time. When she comes out, you say, "Would you please hang up your coat?" If there is still no cooperation, another time out would follow.

What if this girl, for some unknown reason, is in a totally ornery mood today and still doesn't comply? With Start behavior you have more flexibility. Switch from counting to the Docking System and the timer. Set the timer for five minutes. Tell your daughter she has that time to hang up the coat. If she picks it up, fine. Don't say another word. If she doesn't hang the thing up, you have good news and bad news. You'll hang up the coat for her, but you will charge for your services: twenty-five cents for the coat and twenty-five cents for all the aggravation that was just involved in getting her to hang it up. Keep the talking to a minimum, and count whining, arguing, yelling and other forms of testing.

What can you use this version of the 1-2-3 for? Items like brushing teeth, picking up something, or just "Would you please come here for a second?" You are in the kitchen and you need some help for a minute. You can see your ten-year-old son in the other room, lying on the couch, eyes wide open. You say, "Would you please come here?" His response is "I can't. I'm busy."

This kid's about as busy as a large rock. So let's redo this one.

"Would you please come here?"
"I can't. I'm busy."
"That's 1."
"Oh, all right!"

And the reluctant servant enters the room to carry out your bidding.

Simple Requests Revisited

Now let's return to our question about simple requests. What if, in spite of the fact that your voice quality was matter-of-fact, your request was not spur-of-the-moment, and your phrasing was not wishy-washy, your child still does not comply with what you ask him to do? After reading this chapter, you now realize that you have several options.

For example, after your son returned home from school, you told him: "Be sure you change your clothes before you go outside to play." He's been having a snack and playing an electronic game, still in his school clothes, when one of his friends calls him from the back door. Your son calls back that he'll be right out. It doesn't sound as though a different wardrobe is on his mind at all.

Here are some choices you have at this point:

1. Set the timer for ten minutes and tell your son, "I want your clothes changed before the timer goes off." Avoid what we call "shouldy" think-ing—the kind of parental thinking that expects kids to act like adults. If you were into shouldy thinking, you might have said, "I want your clothes changed before the timer goes off. I already told you that. What does it take to get you to listen to me for once? I'm the one who has to do the laundry, you know, and buy you all sorts of new things to wear!"

You could also add a reward or a consequence to the act of changing clothes before the timer goes off. You would not do this every time, but sometimes a strategy like this can "jump-start" the kids into remembering a new behavior. "You change before the timer goes off, you can stay up ten minutes later tonight. If you don't beat the timer, bedtime is ten minutes earlier." Simple, calm, straightforward.

2. Can you use the Docking System here? No, because you can't put his clothes on and charge him for the service. You could, of course, use the Docking System if what you had asked your son to do was take out the garbage. After his first refusal of the refuse, you might simply say, "Do you want to take out the trash or do you want to pay me to do it?"

3. How about natural consequences for our reluctant clothes changer? This tactic is a possibility. The boy who plays outside in his school clothes might be required to wash his outfit as soon as he comes in.

4. Finally, you could consider using counting. Can your son change clothes in two minutes? Maybe. So as the boy is walking out the door—school outfit still on—you simply say, "That's 1." He probably won't know right away what you're talking about, so he'll respond with, "What?" His comment may even be a little ornery.

That's good—make him think a little. You pause, then say, "School clothes." If your son then goes off to his room in a huff to change, fine. You probably don't have to count the huff. If, however, he yells at you, "WHY DO I ALWAYS HAVE TO CHANGE MY IDIOT SCHOOL CLOTHES?! ARE THEY MADE OUT OF GOLD THREADS?!"

Touchy little devil. Pop quiz: What should you do now?

You got it! You say, "That's 2" for testing tactic #2, temper.

Now that you have these Start behavior stategies, you can creatively use them to address many problems you'll have with your children. In fact, once you get going you'll probably come up with some new tactics on your own. And remember, "If any of you lacks wisdom, he should ask God, who gives generously to all without finding fault, and it will be given to him" (James 1:5) Next, let's take a look at how to apply these procedures to some of the most common Start behavior problems parents encounter with their youngsters. You're going to be an expert motivator of children in no time!

Points to Remember...

Your 7 Start Behavior Tactics

1. Praise or positive reinforcement
2. Simple requests
3. Kitchen timers
4. The Docking System
5. Natural consequences
6. Charting
7. A variation of counting

Keep your thinking cap on—and good luck!

Questions for Christian Practice

1. Read Proverbs 22:6, Luke 6:40 and Ephesians 6:4. What kind of training are parents expected to provide their children.

2. What are some specific ways you plan to increase the use of positive reinforcement?

3. What are some ways you can improve your simple requests?

4. List some ways you can use the kitchen timer, the Docking System, and charting with your child to encourage good behavior.

5. Is it difficult sometimes for you to allow natural consequences to occur with your child? Explain, then list one area where natural consequences might be a good option.

14
Up and Out in the Morning

God, treat us kindly. You're our only hope. First thing in the morning, be there for us! When things go bad, help us out!

Isaiah 33:2 (The Message)

Early in the morning my song shall rise to thee. Apparently, the writer of this hymn lyric may not have been a parent. In many homes the environment in the morning is less than spiritual. That's because one of the greatest Start behavior problems is the issue of getting the kids up and out of the house. Most often getting up and out is a problem for grammar-school kids, though it can also be an issue for preschoolers, high school students and even spouses. Morning often brings out the worst in everybody. Many people—both parents and kids—are naturally crabby at that time, and there is the additional pressure of having to get someplace *on time*. The nervousness and emotional thunderstorms that can result have ruined many a parent's day.

For the kids, getting up and out in the morning involves a whole sequence of Start behaviors: out of bed on time, washing up, brushing teeth, getting dressed, eating breakfast and leaving the house with the right equipment. What is required may vary some from family to family, but it's basically the same job.

Believe it or not, these awful morning situations can often be shaped up rather quickly using some of the Start behavior principles we just outlined. Remember, on schoolday mornings counting will not be your primary tactic. But the No-Talking and No-Emotion rules still apply — even if you haven't had your first cup of coffee.

Up and Out for the Little Kids

Very small children in the two-to-five-year-old range are going to need a lot of help and supervision in the morning. These children are not capable of sustaining a positive activity for more than a few minutes, and most of them will not even think of what needs to be done to get out of the house. You're going to have to help two- and three-year-olds get dressed and wash up. You'll also be responsible for remembering anything the children have to take with them. And while you're doing all this, you want to praise lavishly whatever positive efforts the kids make.

Four- and five-year-olds will often respond to the use of very primitive, basic charts. The chart may have only two or three items on it. These charts can also be combined with kitchen timers to produce an effective motivational system. A chart for a preschooler might look something like this:

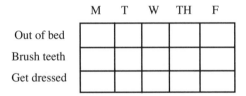

	M	T	W	TH	F
Out of bed					
Brush teeth					
Get dressed					

Set the timer for 15 minutes and give the child a cue that it's time to get started. Many of the little ones are already out of bed, so that item on the chart has been successfully completed. Whatever other tasks the youngster finishes before the timer goes off are recognized with special stickers.

With older kids in the primary grades, the chart may have four or five items on it and the timer may or may not be necessary. For each task, the child earns her favorite sticker for a super job and her next favorite sticker for a good job. No sticker at all means "You blew it today, better luck tomorrow!" The application of the stickers, of course, should be acompanied by a lot of praise: "Good job!" or "Wow, you did it in only twelve minutes!"

In some families, breakfast and TV must wait until the child is totally ready to leave the house—washed, dressed and packed. The breakfast, entertainment and praise serve as reinforcers for the child's successful Start behavior.

What about fighting, teasing, whining or other Stop behavior in the morning? Stop behavior should be counted as usual. If there is time for a time out, don't hesitate to use time outs. If there is not enough time, consider using time out alternatives. "Guys, that's 3. Bedtime is fifteen minutes earlier for both of you tonight. OK, let's get in the car."

Up and Out for Older Kids

For children nine years old and up (including high school age), our up-and-out program involves some drastic alterations in the morning routine. These alterations will often shock the kids into being much more responsible for themselves, but be forewarned: These changes also require extreme self-restraint on the part of moms and dads.

Before explaining the new regime, we remind parents that—believe it or not—most kids want to go to school and would be embarrassed if they were late or didn't show up at all. Parents often don't realize their children feel this way for two reasons: (1) the kids goof off in the morning instead of getting ready and (2) the kids are able to dilly-dally precisely because their parents have habitually taken *all* the responsibility for their youngsters' making it to school on time.

Now that way of thinking is going to change—in both children and parents. Here's how the new procedure works. You explain to the kids that from now on it will be their responsibility—not yours—to get up and out in the morning. *You will neither supervise them nor nag them.* If you have been waking them up, you will wake them up only once from now on. A better system is to get an alarm clock and show the child how to use it. Explain to the kids that if they go back to sleep after your one

> **Quik Tip...**
>
> Tell your older kids that from now on, getting up and out in the morning is going to be their responsibility—totally. You will neither supervise nor nag them. Your children will not at first believe you are serious, but they **will** believe you are serious after you've let them get burned a few times. What's your chief job in all this? It's keeping quiet.

wake-up call or after the alarm goes off, you will not wake them again and they will definitely have a problem.

You make it clear to the kids that getting up, getting dressed, washing up, eating breakfast and leaving on time will be their job—totally. If you wish, you can chart the kids on how well they do getting up and out, but, other than casual conversation, you will not say anything to them.

Your children will not believe that you are serious, because they will find it completely incomprehensible that you would ever allow them to get to school late (you may have trouble with that concept, too). So guess what? You are going to have to make believers out of them.

This new system relies on natural consequences. If the kids dilly-dally in the morning, they are going to run into trouble somewhere. The trouble may be with the other kids in the car pool, who are now afraid that they are going to be late because of your son or daughter (can you stand that?). Or the trouble may come from the child's having to explain to a principal or teacher why he was late and has no parental note excusing him. Most kids don't want these kinds of problems, so we use the threat of these natural consequences to help shape them up.

Some parents can't stand this routine. It drives some grownups crazy to watch their kids fooling around when the bus or car pool ride is coming in five minutes. These are the moments when extreme parental self-restraint is called for. You will want to talk, nag, argue or scream. I've had to ask many parents to take their coffee, retire to the bedroom and not watch the impending disaster.

Breakfast is optional for these older children. You can put some food out if that was your usual routine before, but *you can't remind the kids to eat it.* It's better if the kids just get what they want for themselves. Children won't die from missing breakfast. When they leave, you say nothing about coats, hats or gloves, unless there is danger of frostbite.

What you are doing with this new up-and-out arrangement is teaching the kids responsibility and invoking a sacred rule of psychology: Sometimes Learning the Hard Way Is the Best Way to Learn. The lessons sink in more when kids get burned a few times than they do when they simply hear a lecture. So you have to be willing to let the kids get burned. *Don't even start this procedure unless you are convinced you are ready for the strain and—more important—that you can keep quiet.*

It usually takes no more than five days for the child to shape up and successfully get up and out on his own. During that five day period your youngster will probably be late to school a few times and will feel embarrassed. He will have had the experience of suddenly realizing at 7:50 that he's not dressed and that Mom didn't remind him that his ride was coming at 8:00. He may have gotten to school and realized he forgot his math book because he was late leaving. He may also have blown his stack at his mother a few times (and been counted!) because she didn't provide any reminders or any excuse notes.

Kids have four main ways of getting to school: car pool, bus, walking, or riding bikes. When you are within walking distance of the school, of course, this up-and-out program is the easiest. With car pools or bus, you may have to drive the kids if they don't make their connection. Don't rush, however; make sure they still get to school late. Most kids will not get dependent on your driving, especially if they're late all the time anyway. If you do have to drive the kids, remember not to lecture them on the way to school.

These negative experiences have quite a bit of impact on most kids. If the parents are consistent, don't talk and let the kids get burned, the children will shape up in a few days. No "I told you so" comments are allowed. Then things will be much more peaceful at home in the morning and the kids will be much more responsible.

Some parents have used charting along with our natural consequences program. If you decide to do this, make sure you praise good performances ("It's so much easier with you getting yourself up in the morning!") and review the chart at least once a week. You *can* discuss the issue, listen, give brief suggestions or make modifications at times other than when the kids are getting ready in the morning.

Take a Deep Breath

Many parents, before they've used this gutsy procedure, think their kids will be indifferent. Moms and dads think their children really won't care whether or not they get to school on time. Part of the reason the grownups think this is the case is because the youngsters have said so.

Never believe a child who says "I don't care." He usually means the opposite.

If you are skeptical about this up-and-out procedure, consider trying this arrangement and see what happens. Make sure you're ready, though, before you start. Most kids—not all, but most—will shape up. The kids will get up and out on their own. The most important rules are to keep quiet and be willing to let the children get burned—more than once, if necessary. You may want to let the school know what you're doing. Most teachers and principals will cooperate with you, especially if you explain your purpose and label the procedure "independence training."

What if you just don't think you can stand it? You have some other Start behavior tools. Consider charting, perhaps with artificial reinforcers, and the use of a kitchen timer. Since these kids are older, you might also entertain the idea of discussing your morning routines at a family meeting (see Chapter 19). One way or another, though, it is absolutely critical for everyone to start out the day on a positive note. Adults take bad memories from unsuccessful mornings to work with them, and kids can take those same lousy memories to school.

If you are successful using natural consequences? Relax and enjoy your kids, another cup of coffee, and the peace and quiet.

Good luck!

Points to Remember...

Summary: Up and Out

1. For preschoolers, give the kids a lot of help and praise.
2. For young children (six to nine), use some basic Start behavior tactics, such as praise, timers and charting.
3. For older kids, take a deep breath and try natural consequences!

Questions for Christian Practice

1. Read Psalm 59:16, 143:8, and Lamentations 3:22-23. How do these verses compare to your current morning routine?

2. What is the most difficult aspect of your morning routine?

3. If you plan to use a chart for morning behaviors, what will it include? How long will the kids have to complete their tasks, and how will you check their progress?

4. What are your concerns about using natural consequences to help your older child learn how to get up in the morning?

5. Once your children have mastered the morning routine, what could you do to offer them some encouragement (family prayer time, Bible reading for the day, etc.)?

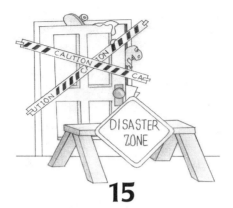

15

Cleaning Rooms, Picking Up and Chores

Whatever you do, work at it with all your heart, as working for the Lord, not for men.

Colossians 3:23

Wouldn't it be great if children were born with a desire to be neat and organized? Unfortunately, this is not the case. In fact, it seems that most kids are naturally messy. Take a look in most kids' rooms and this becomes quite obvious. Your stomach may churn with distaste when you view the scene of destruction and chaos that is your daughter's bedroom. You forgot what color the carpet was. The cat was last seen in there three weeks ago.

> "Barbara, GET UP HERE RIGHT THIS MINUTE!"
> "What?"
> "LOOK AT THIS ROOM! I can't even see the CARPET!
>   How am I supposed to do your clothes?"

Since picking up and cleaning rooms are not natural traits of kids, children must be trained to accomplish these tasks. At first, your children will work at their chores because you as a parent demand it. However, the goal is for your child to eventually take personal responsibility in this area. They should do this for themselves and to honor God. Colossians 3:23 encourages all of us to work hard at whatever we do not just to please others, but to please God. By training your children to clean their room, pick-up, and complete their chores, you will be helping them learn to please God with their work.

How can you train your children to accomplish these goals? By this time you shouldn't have to be reminded that you won't get the kids to complete this unpleasant chore by nagging or delivering the lecture, "The Seven Reasons Why It's Easier on Me for You to Have a Clean Room."

Instead, you have several options. If you're creative, you can probably come up with several more. Here are some good ones.

Strategies for Cleaning Bedrooms

Option 1: Close the Door and Don't Look

Having a clean room is not a life-or-death matter. We know of no research that indicates that kids who didn't keep their rooms neat grew up to be homeless people, mentally unbalanced or have a higher divorce rate. Besides, whose room is it? You don't have to live in it, so why not just ask the child to keep the door closed so you don't have to be aggravated.

Most parents don't like this idea, but before you dismiss the Close-the-Door-and-Don't-Look method, ask yourself one question: Do you have a child with a significant behavioral or emotional problem, such as ADHD, learning disability, anxiety or depression? If you have a handicapped child or one who's very difficult, why add another set of problems? Imagine your daughter hates school, hates homework, has no friends, feels lousy most of the time and fights with her brother constantly. Should you also get after her about the stuff lying around on her bedroom floor? You need to straighten out your priorities, because you have bigger fish to fry.

Option 1 is quite legitimate for some families, but there are two problems with this procedure: (1) most parents find the notion unacceptable, and (2) dirty dishes and dirty laundry, which can't be ignored.

If you don't want to use Option 1, more suggestions will follow in the next sections of this chapter. As for dirty dishes and dirty clothes, you can try almost any other Start behavior tactic: a timer, charting or the 1-2-3 (if the dishes or clothes can be picked up in less than two minutes) can be helpful. Remember to praise compliance from time to time with older kids, and frequently with younger children.

Some parents whose kids are older simply tell them that any clothes that don't make it to the laundry or hamper simply don't get washed. Then the child has to wash them herself. Those are examples of natural consequences. The Docking System can also be considered. You go and get the dirty clothes or dishes from the room, but you charge your son or daughter for your labor. You'll feel better about having to do the job. Make sure you keep your mouth shut about the whole operation and keep the fees reasonable.

Option 2: The Weekly Cleanup Routine

This procedure is a favorite with many moms and dads. With the Weekly Cleanup, the kids have to clean their rooms only once a week, but according to your specifications. You might explain that the following has to be done: pick up, put clothes in hamper, make bed, maybe vacuum. A specific day and time, such as Saturday morning, is chosen and the youngster is not allowed to go outside, play or do anything else until his room is done and you've checked him out. You can check him out by using a chart if you wish.

Cleaning the room is a Start behavior, and you will be rewarding the child immediately after the room cleaning with both freedom as well as praise. If artificial reinforcers are necessary, these rewards will be tallied or recorded at checkout time.

Many parents have tried something like the Weekly Cleanup Routine, but the grownups often ruin the whole procedure by getting into an argument with the child at checkout. Never argue about what needs to be done; make the specifications clear in the first place. For example:

"I'm done with my room. Can I go out now?"
"Your bed's not finished."
"Whadda ya mean? That's good enough."
(Mom turns to walk away.)
"What's the matter with it?"
"That's 1."
"Oh, for Pete's sake!!" (Goes to finish bed.)

This Mom had already explained before that the bed has to be reasonably neatly made, so there was no need for further talk. Her son, though, starts testing, using the badgering tactic, and, after ignoring the badgering once, Mom uses the 1-2-3. If the youngster winds up back in his room with a 3 count and a time out, that's perfect—he'll have five minutes to make his bed properly.

Option 3: Daily Charting

For parents who are more fastidious about cleanliness, the child's room can be charted every day using either a star or sticker system (for younger kids) or a 1-through-5 rating system (for older kids). The child should be informed that your room rating will take place at the same time every day, such as every night right before bed, though bedtime ratings are not such a good idea if they typically aggravate everybody. Keep in mind that expecting a neat room every day is probably asking for a lot of trouble. So if you insist on this perverse procedure, be nice! Use a lot of praise if the job is done well, and don't expect perfection.

Tactics for Picking Up

Let me make one thing perfectly clear: The Close-the-Door-and-Don't-Look method applies only to the kids' rooms. The scheme does not apply to the rest of your house! It does not mean the children can leave your kitchen, family room, dining room or hallways constantly cluttered with all their things. As all parents know, kitchen counters and tables are such convenient dumping grounds!

In our research, not picking up after yourself was the main Start behavior problem reported by parents of young children. You certainly can't close a door and not look when the entire house is involved. Here are some ideas.

Kitchen Timer and Docking System

These two Start behavior tactics can be very useful in getting the house picked up—especially when you can't avoid having to straighten up on the spur of the moment. When the job has to be done right away, the timer is helpful for picking up rooms, such as family rooms and kitchens.

If a surprise guest is coming over, you may not have much time to play around:

"Hey, kids. Mr. and Mrs. Johnson are coming over in 45
    minutes. I'll need all your stuff out of the kitchen by then.
    I'm setting the timer."

When using the timer like this, it's perfectly OK to add an artificial reward if the room is done within a certain time, or even an artificial punishment if it's not. Just be sure not to use artificials for everything you ask the kids to do. Your praise should be enough reward most of the time—and don't forget that part of a child's satisfaction when you praise him is knowing that he did something that made you happy.

The Garbage Bag Method

This procedure has been a favorite of parents for many years. The deal is this. You first encourage the children, as much as possible, not to leave their stuff lying around the house. You're not going to expect perfection. "Stuff" includes clothes, DVDs, books, papers, toys, shoes, pens, comics, electronic games, videos, fossils and so on.

Next, you tell the kids that at a certain time every day, their things have to be removed from the public areas of the house and returned to their

Quik Tip...

Your kids do not have a right to mess up your entire house! Tell the children that by a certain time every day, anything of theirs that you find lying around will be confiscated and unavailable to them until a certain time the following day. Pick up the kids' things without grumbling or lecturing. You'll soon find that before the magic hour comes each day, the youngsters will be scurrying around to salvage their possessions.

bedrooms. Maybe you pick 8:00 as the cutoff time. Anything left out after 8:00 will be picked up by you and put into a big garbage bag or some other container, and the child will lose the right to use those items until 6:00 the following day. You can set the times however you want.

Some parents threaten to actually throw away the things they find that are not put away. There are two problems with this notion. First, if you do throw away some of your children's possessions, that's pretty harsh. After all, they're just kids and don't have an inherent desire to pick up after themselves. Second, it's likely you won't really throw the stuff away, you'll just go blustering around about that possibility and about how unfair your life is. In this case, you are simply making a useless, empty threat, and the kids will catch on to you right away.

Imagine you're using the garbage bag routine and have picked 8:00 as the cutoff time. At 7:50 you remind seven-year-old Caitlin that her things need to be picked up. She doesn't respond because she doesn't really think you'll do anything. At 8:05, however, when you quietly begin walking around with a large, plastic bag and have already claimed five of her prize posessions, Caitlin becomes a believer. She runs around frantically grabbing whatever of hers she can find before you get to it and yelling, "This is stupid! This isn't fair!"

You consider counting her screaming, but you don't. You put the bag away in your bedroom closet. The following night at 7:50, when you say "Clean up time!" Caitlin scurries around retrieving her things and then she takes them to her bedroom. You say, "Good job, Caitlin—it looks real nice in here!"

The 55-Gallon Drum

This next plan is one that I cannot take credit for. The idea was described to me by a lady I spoke with on the phone many years ago. She told me that picking up around her house had never been a problem. This resourceful mother kept a 55-gallon, metal drum in the garage, which was right next to her kitchen. Whenever she would find anything of her children's that was out of place, she would simply put the items in the metal drum.

This procedure had become so routine with her four boys, that whenever one of the kids couldn't find something of his, he would simply look in the drum. For example, her second oldest came running into the kitchen one day and exclaimed, "Mom, I can't find my gym shoes. Are they in the drum?" "Yes," was mother's reply, and the incident was over.

You say you don't happen to have a 55-gallon drum handy or your kids couldn't reach in there if you did? A large box will do fine.

Chores

By now you could probably write this section on chores yourself, so we only need to make a few points. First of all, praise your little ones (five and under) whenever they help out, but don't expect them to be able to remember or to sustain work projects for more than a few minutes. Second, when the kids are approximately six and over, consider using the Family Meeting (see Chapter 19) to discuss and divide up the jobs that regularly need to be done. This planning will help you avoid the Curse of the Spontaneous Request, which we mentioned earlier.

Third, charting is an excellent tactic for chores. The chart serves both as a reminder of what needs to be done, as well as a record of how well the task was accomplished. When charting chores, consider trying only natural reinforcers (praise, the chart itself and job satisfaction) initially. See how far you get with naturals and only use artificial rewards (allowance, points, etc.) if you're not getting anywhere because the task is so obnoxious or foreign to your youngster.

Fourth, the Docking System is also perfectly suited to chores. If the kids don't do what they're supposed to, you quietly do it for them and they pay you. Keep in mind that the payment should not be accompanied by a parental lecture about responsibility. Also be forewarned that some kids will be happy to simply pay you for doing their jobs, and their chore-completion behavior will not improve. What do you do in this case? You can up the ante—they pay more for you to do the chore. Or you can just take the money and run. Consider this an introduction for your child to the workings of a service economy: You don't get free service, you pay for it. There's a lesson in that for your kids.

One final word about pets. Caring for an animal is obviously a chore. When they are overwhelmed with excitement about getting a cat or dog, most kids don't realize that eventually having this animal will mean having to regularly complete boring tasks, such as feeding, watering, cleaning up and brushing. When it comes to pets, our Start behavior tactics are not all equally helpful. Praise, the use of a timer, and charting can all be useful, of course. Natural consequences is inappropriate, however, because this method endangers the animal. Perhaps the best method for pets is the Docking System, because you can care for the pet while your child is learning to be more responsible.

With regard to pets, however, the best advice for parents is this: Don't get any animal that you don't want to take care of yourself.

Points to Remember...

Parents' Favorites

For CLEANING ROOMS: The Weekly Cleanup Routine
For PICKING UP: The Garbage Bag Method
For CHORES (except homework): The Docking System

Questions for Christian Practice

1. Read Genesis 39:1-6. Why did Potiphar put Joseph in charge? How can you help your child be successful through work?

2. What is your current plan for cleaning rooms, picking up, and chores? Is it working well?

3. Which room cleaning option do you like most? Why?

4. Which tactics for cleaning up will work best for your children?

5. Outline a family meeting to discuss your new plan for cleaning rooms, picking up and chores.

16
Mealtimes

So whether you eat or drink or whatever you do, do it all for the glory of God.

1 Corinthians 10:31

The Bible encourages us to be thankful and glorify God in all that we do. This can sometimes be a challenge at mealtimes. They say mealtimes are supposed to be a time for family togetherness and family bonding. Dinnertime is a time to open up, talk about your day and enjoy everybody's company. Unfortunately, it all too often happens that when you mix together some general childhood fidgetiness, a little sibling rivalry, a finicky eater or two and tired parents, you've got a recipe for an unpleasant time.

The Case of Picky Pete

Here's a situation most parents have experienced at one time or another. It's suppertime at the Jenkins' house. Peter, however, is not a happy camper. He's picking unenthusiastically at his food:

> Mom: "Come on, Peter. Let's get going."
> Peter: "I'm not hungry."
> Dad: "What did you have to eat after school?"
> Peter: "Not that much."

Dad: "Then how come you're not eating?"

Peter: "I am eating!"

Mom: "No you're not!"

Peter: "We never have anything I like."

Silence. Parents look at each other and continue eating.

Peter: "Why do I have to eat this stuff?"

Mom: "Because, you know, you want to grow up to be big—strong."

Peter: "But I don't like any of it."

Mom: "OK, if you don't finish, there will be no dessert and nothing else to eat before bed. Do you understand?"

Alicia (Peter's sister): "I like what we're having."

Peter: "Oh, shut up!"

Dad: "Peter, you've got five minutes to finish."

Peter: "Dogfood's better than this junk!"

Dad: "Go up to your room, right now, young man! That's no way to talk to anyone!!"

Peter departs.

This scene is anything but a warm and friendly family interaction. This episode has all the elements for disaster: one picky eater, two fighting sibs and two weary parents who are talking too much and asking silly questions. Here are several ideas to help avoid this kind of trouble.

> Try this with your finicky eaters. Give the kids super-small portions and then set the timer for twenty minutes. If the children finish before the timer goes off, they get their dessert. You may not nag or prompt—the timer will do that for you.

Small Portions and a Kitchen Timer

Do you have fussy eaters like Picky Pete? Get out a kitchen timer and set it for twenty minutes when you all sit down at the table. Tell the kids they have to finish their dinner in that time. If they do finish the meal in twenty minutes, they get their dessert.

When starting the kitchen timer method, initially give your hard-to-please children very small portions of foods they don't like. Even ridiculously small, if necessary, such as three peas, a tablespoon of scalloped potatoes, two bites of pork chop. Research shows that children who are exposed to new foods, but not forced to eat them, will often come around and start to enjoy some of the more exotic possibilities. That result is a lot more healthy in the long run for them.

If the kids goof around or fight at the dinner table, they get counted. If anyone hits a count of three, he is timed out for five minutes while the twenty minutes on the timer keeps on ticking. Don't do any prodding or nagging about eating, such as, "Come on now, don't forget the timer's ticking" or "Quit that goofing around and get down to eating, young man!" (How are you going to finish your own meal if you're talking all the time?)

You are probably also aware by now that you would not count the kids for not eating. Eating is a Start behavior, not a Stop behavior. What will help prompt the children to wolf down the chow? The timer: tick, tick, tick. You can, though, praise the kids when they do eat.

What if the timer rings and there is still food on the plates? No dessert—at least yet. The plate goes into the kitchen and onto the counter. Cover the plate with plastic wrap. After one half hour has expired, the children have the right to finish the meal if they wish. The food can be nuked quickly in the microwave if necessary. If the youngsters don't ever eat the rest of their meal, that's fine—but still no dessert. Some parents throw the rest of the child's dinner down the disposal when the timer hits twenty minutes, but this procedure seems a little extreme.

Stay on your toes when a hungry little tot who didn't finish her dinner puts the hit on you later for some dessert:

"I'm ready for my ice cream now."
"You'll have to finish your dinner first, honey."
"It's all cold."
"We'll just heat it in the microwave for a few seconds and it'll
     be good as new."
"I didn't like it anyway. I just want a little ice cream."
"Now you know the rules, dear, you have to finish what's on
     your plate first. Remember, we didn't give you that much in
     the first place."

"I never get anything!"

"What are you talking about—you never get anything?! That's
  enough of that! Either finish your dinner or stop bugging me!"

"I hate you!"

This interaction was an unfortunate waste of time and was also very
hard on this relationship. The conversation should have gone like this:

"I'm ready for my ice cream now."

"You'll have to finish your dinner first, honey."

"It's all cold."

"We'll just heat it in the microwave for a few seconds and it'll
  be good as new."

"I didn't like it anyway. I want just a little ice cream."

"That's 1."

"Then I'll go to bed starving!" (Walks away)

Mom did much better. There was no useless, little-adult talking, and
then mother ignored her daughter's martyrdom.

The 3-out-of-4 Rule

Let's return to the case of Picky Pete. Imagine that Peter's parents sit down,
review the mealtime situation, and come up with a new plan. Mom and
Dad explain the new deal to their son: If Peter eats three out of four items
on his plate, the boy can have his dessert. The serving sizes will be smaller
and Peter has to at least taste the one thing he doesn't choose to eat.

The first meal under the new regime goes well. Even though they are
a bit nervous, both parents avoid any anxious prompting. Peter finishes
his smaller portions of pork, mashed potatoes and peas. After tasting it,
he forgoes the salad. He gets ice cream for dessert.

After the mealtime overhaul, the first week passes without any
unpleasant incidents. Peter and his parents actually enjoy one another's
company; the dinner table conversation is spirited and friendly.

"Pete, how was that movie you saw with your friend?"

"Oh, cool! You guys gotta see it!"

"You really think we'd like it at our advanced ages?"

"Oh, yeah! Let's go—I'll go see it again."

"Well, if your mother's willing, it might be possible."

"Mom, you gotta go. It's so neat! There's this one part where..."

That's the way meals should be. What if Peter and Alicia start fighting? They would both be counted. In our original scene, it would go something like this:

Peter: "But I don't like any of it."

Mom: "OK, if you don't finish, there will be no dessert and nothing else to eat before bed. Do you understand?"

Alicia (Peter's sister): "I like what we're having."

Peter: "Oh, shut up!"

Mom: "That's 1 for each of you."

Some of you may wonder why Alicia should be counted. All she did was say, "I like what we're having." The answer: It's all in her timing.

The Divide-and-Conquer Routine

Many families seem to feel that there is a federal law that dictates that every family eat supper together each and every night of the year. This is the time, the experts claim, for "family togetherness" and for each person to "share his or her day" with everyone else. Sometimes, however, it seems that dinner simply becomes a time for everyone to share his *hostility* toward everyone else. Tempers as well as appetites can be lost.

What can a parent do to improve this situation? One solution, obviously, is not to eat together every night. Though some people consider this sacrilegious, it sure beats fighting all the time. Now you only have to fight every other night! Seriously, consider feeding the kids first or letting them eat in front of the TV for once. Or, now and then, let the kids eat wherever they want to, as long as they bring back their dishes. Then later Mom and Dad can eat in the kitchen or have a peaceful dinner together.

Key Concepts...

Who says you have to eat dinner together every single night of the year? Consider having some special nights where each person eats wherever she wishes. Or—better yet—have some nights where one parent takes one child out to eat. It's different and it's fun!

Another idea is for each parent to periodically take one child out to dinner as a kind of special occasion. This one-parent, one-child setup is one that the kids love. It's also one where sibling rivalry is not possible, so the parent is much more relaxed and able to enjoy herself.

Think about dinnertime. Eating supper should be a pleasant experience. In fact, with most children eating is a natural and enjoyable function that doesn't require much parental intervention. With a little planning you can enjoy your evenings a lot more.

Points to Remember...

How to make mealtimes more pleasant and more fun:
1. Small portions and a kitchen timer
2. The 3-out-of-4 Rule
3. The Divide-and-Conquer Routine

Questions for Christian Practice

1. Read I Thessalonians 5:11 and Hebrews 3:13. How do these verses apply to an ideal family mealtime? Is your family dinner a place of encouragement? Why or why not?

2. If you have a Picky Pete, describe how you've handled him at mealtimes.

3. Which ideas from this chapter do you plan to try?

4. How do you feel about occasionally using the Divide-and-Conquer Routine?

5. How can you encourage your children during your new more enjoyable mealtime?

17

Homework and Practicing

The plans of the diligent lead to profit as surely as haste leads to poverty.

Proverbs 21:5

God's word is full of admonitions to be diligent and to work hard. Many verses in Proverbs emphasize the wisdom of hard work and the foolishness of laziness. Unfortunately, few children are born with a biblical work ethic. Instead, parents must work to instill these habits in their children. One area of work for children is homework. However, homework civil wars can make school nights miserable for the whole family. A typical scene involves junior sitting at the kitchen table after dinner staring out the window with a sour look on his face. The boy's favorite sister, who completed her homework years ago, sits in the other room, smugly watching TV. Mom and dad check into the kitchen every five or ten minutes to badger the reluctant scholar.

In some families, schoolwork battles can go on for three or four hours per night. Everyone begins to dread the evening, relationships are strained severely, and the child in question learns to hate schoolwork. There are no easy answers to the homework problem; children's needs vary depending upon their intelligence and the presence of handicaps such as learning disabilities and Attention Deficit Disorder. There are ways, though, of making things more tolerable and more productive.

Routine Is Critical

First of all, the worst mistake you can make is to ask your child—just when you happen to think about it—if he has homework. This is an example of a spontaneous request, and your question is sure to provoke hostility. Homework should be a daily *routine*—done at the same time and in the same place as much as possible.

One of the best ways of setting things up is to have the child come home, get a snack, goof around for about thirty to forty-five minutes and then sit down in a quiet spot and try to finish his schoolwork before dinner. Then the whole evening is free for the youngster. The evening will also then be free of homework hassles for you too. For many, but not all, children, afternoon is preferable to evening for homework because the child has more energy.

Don't let your young student do academic work with the TV on. The television is always out to get your attention. Believe it or not, however, music from a CD or headset may be fine. For many young children and teens, music provides consistent background noise, usually is not new to the child and often tends to block out other household noises.

Natural Consequences

If you are having trouble with homework for the first time—say with a fourth grader—consider trying the natural consequences approach first. That means you do nothing: Keep quiet and see if the child and the teacher can work things out. Too many parents get too anxious way too soon about their children's schoolwork, with the result that the grownup prematurely takes charge and doesn't give the youngster a chance to learn—and exercise—true responsibility.

Let your daughter, for example, explain to *her* teacher why *her* work was not completed. And when your daughter later complains to you about how irritated her teacher was with her for not turning her homework in, instead of saying, "I told you so," say, "That must have been embarrassing for you, but I'm sure you'll do better tomorrow." If this approach doesn't seem to be working after a few weeks, then switch to some of the other alternatives listed below.

Natural consequences is obviously not the method to use, however, if you have been having homework problems for years and years. With chronic problems, you will need to take a closer look at why your child is having such a hard time. Children with learning disabilities and attention deficit problems, for instance, not only need a well-thought-out daily homework routine, these kids may also benefit from tutoring, treatment or other academic accomodations.

Assignment Sheets

Assignment sheets or assignment notebooks can be extremely helpful for kids who have homework troubles. Assignment notebooks tell you exactly what work is due for each subject, which—among other benefits—helps prevent lying about homework. Some schools have even instituted Internet-based "Homework Hotlines," where forgetful-but-fortunate kids can log on after hours to find out what their assignments are.

Part of the idea of the assignment sheet, of course, is that after the child does the work, the parents can check her productions against the list of items to be done. If this is the procedure you are considering, you should routinely include our next two homework procedures: the PNP Method and the Rough Checkout. Failure to do so will result in unnecessary conflict and misery.

The PNP Method

Suppose your daughter has just completed her midweek spelling pretest. There are ten words on the list, and she spelled nine correctly and misspelled one. When she brings you her paper, your job, naturally, is to first point out to her the word she spelled wrong. Right?

Wrong! PNP stands for "Positive-Negative-Positive." *Whenever a youngster brings any piece of schoolwork to you, the first thing out of your mouth must be something positive*—some type of praise. You might, for instance, simply praise the child for remembering to show you her work. After saying something nice about the child's effort, you may then make a negative comment, if it's absolutely necessary. Finally, you conclude your insightful remarks with something positive again. So the procedure is Positive-Negative (if necessary)-Positive.

Using the spelling pretest as an example, you might first say something like, "Gee, you spelled 'consideration' correctly. That's a pretty hard word. And you also got 'appearance' right. That's another long one! In fact, there's only one word on here that I can see you didn't get. Not bad at all." You might stop here and try to kill your daughter with suspense. See if she's dying to find out what the wrong word is. If she's not, you can tell her. End the conversation with another positive comment.

Remember the rule: Every time she brings you some work to check, the first thing you say must be positive. That type of response will help bring her back again and again. Kids will never want to bring you anything if you follow your natural human inclinations and shoot from the hip with criticism.

The Rough Checkout

Our next idea, the Rough Checkout, will also help to make your evenings a lot more pleasant. The Rough Checkout notion is based on the fact that 8:00 in the evening is no time for scholastic perfection. You have worked all day, and your child has also put in just about the equivalent of a day on a full-time job—before she even started her homework!

Unless there is some major indication to the contrary, if your daughter's schoolwork is anywhere near 80 percent neat, correct and thorough, consider calling it a day and consider the job done. Let your youngster and teacher continue worrying about the assignment tomorrow if they want to.

Quik Tip...

The first thing out of your mouth when your child shows you her homework must be something positive—even if it's just that she brought her work to you. And remember: 8:00 p.m. is no time for academic perfection!

This advice is doubly true for ADD or LD children who are already having a tough enough time with school. You can also adjust your Rough Checkout criteria to your child's overall achievement level. If, for example, your child is generally an excellent student (A-B average), you might consider raising the required neat, correct and thorough percentage to 90 or more.

I learned this advice the hard way. A mother once came into my office reporting that her twelve-year-old son was getting more depressed, more irritable and more distant from everyone in the family. It turned out that homework was a major problem for this boy every night. The lad would finish his assignments and bring them to his father for checkout. That was the good news. The bad news was that if the work was not absolutely perfect, Dad would tear it all up and make his son start over!

When asked how many times — on the average — the Dad was tearing up the kid's homework, the mother said about three times per evening. No wonder the boy was getting demoralized.

I insisted on seeing the father. Dad blustered into the office insisting that his son was going to learn to do things right the first time and that he should try to be the best, etc., etc. I replied that the boy was indeed learning a lot: He was learning to hate schoolwork, to hate his father, to hate evenings and to hate himself. I further added that if this nightly routine was continued, it would produce a high school dropout within four years. The father — somewhat reluctantly — agreed to stop his ridiculous and tyrannical homework procedure. That was the end of that and, not surprisingly, this father also started enjoying his evenings more.

So, if your youngster's work is by far mostly neat, correct and complete — but not perfect — consider the PNP procedure. Don't tell the child, of course, that his schoolwork is superb, because it's not. Just say that the work is good and praise some specific parts of what he has done. Perfectionist parents who squirm at this suggestion need to stay in touch with the emotional realities of childhood.

Charting for Homework

A daily charting system can be a godsend when it comes to improving academic work and decreasing homework hostilities. This is especially true when charting is combined with the Rough Checkout and Positive-Negative-Positive methods and when spur-of-the-moment homework requests are avoided. Here's an easy arrangement that can be used.

Since it's usually the older kids who have trouble with homework, a five-point scale instead of stickers can be used on the chart. Five is the highest mark and one is the lowest mark. A child can earn one point for each of the following things:

• Neat:	1 point
• Correct:	1 point
• Thorough:	1 point
• No complaining:	1 point
• Starting on your own at the right time without being reminded:	<u>1 point</u>
Total possible score:	5 points

The kids can get each of the first three points by doing better than whatever approximate percentage of neatness, correctness and completeness you have required according to your Rough Checkout rules. The no-complaining point is earned if the youngster doesn't whine or grouse about having to do his schoolwork.

Quik Tip...
When charting homework performance using our 5-point system, the fifth point is the Magic Point. A child earns the fifth point for starting his schoolwork at the right time without being reminded. That's half the battle!

The last point is the crucial one. We sometimes call the fifth point the Magic Point, because if you can get a child to start his work on his own, in a timely fashion and without being reminded, the battle is more than half won! You can also set up friendly incentive games with this last Magic Point. For example, three days in a row of starting on your own at the proper time earns a bonus point. Or starting more than fifteen minutes early and finishing in a reasonable amount of time earns two bonus points.

Put on your thinking cap and see what other schemes you can come up with. The possibilities are endless, and playing around with the Magic Point helps accomplish the impossible—making homework more fun.

Remember that for many kids with academic handicaps, you may very well have to use artificial reinforcers to help motivate the child over the homework hurdle. Your successful young scholar, for example, might earn a special outing with you, a special meal, part of his allowance, or time on a new game for posting a certain number of points during the week. Different rewards may require different numbers of points. Check back to our list of rewards on page 135.

Also, don't forget that kitchen timer when dealing with homework.

For instance, a timer can be used to help break up the work into smaller, more manageable fifteen-to-twenty-minute pieces. A timer also helps keep kids on task. If your child complains that the ticking bothers him, use some kind of sand hourglass or a quiet LCD device.

Practicing

When I was young my parents required that I take music lessons from time to time. As you can easily imagine, one of my least favorite memories is having to come in from playing baseball out in the street in order to practice the piano or clarinet. So here's a warning to all you parents from a former kid: *Sophisticated and well-conceived parenting technology is necessary to get children to practice regularly.*

The tactics for getting kids to practice follow the same logic as those for homework. Avoid spontaneous requests and consider natural consequences first if a child is just starting out. Some of these music teachers are downright scary, and many children would not dare come to their lesson unprepared. If natural consequences don't work, try charting with or without artificial rewards.

The PNP method also applies to practicing. Make sure your comments start with positive reinforcement, add negative remarks if it's absolutely necessary, then conclude with the positive again.

Charting also can help a lot with practicing. For some kids just putting on the chart the number of minutes they practiced can be enough to keep them going. For others, artificial reinforcers may be necessary. Keep in mind that points for not complaining and—especially—for starting on your own without being reminded are very helpful. We're trying to reinforce not only musical ability but also attitude.

Now that the homework and practicing are out of the way, it's time for bed!

Points to Remember...

Homework Helpers

1. Routine is CRITICAL!
2. Natural consequences
3. The Positive-Negative-Positive (PNP) Method

4. The Rough Checkout
5. Charting

Questions for Christian Practice

1. Read Proverbs 24:30-34, Proverbs 21:25 and 6:6-11. What is the Bible's view on work?

2. Describe your current homework and/or practice routine. Is it working well? How can you improve the routine?

3. How do you feel about first trying natural consequences for homework success?

4. Are you more negative or positive when you approach homework with your child? How can using the PNP help improve your approach to homework?

5. Do you think the Rough Checkout or Charting will be useful in your approach to homework or practicing? Explain.

18
Bedtime and Nighttime Waking

On my bed I remember you; I think of you through the watches of the night.

Psalm 63:6

The Psalmist who wrote Psalm 63:6 describes night as a peaceful place. Remembering God in the evening brings thoughts of serenity and calm to the close of the day. However, for many families evenings are far from peaceful. In fact, putting the kids to bed is a daily nightmare for some parents. Although bedtime may technically be 9:00, at 10:30 the children are still wandering around asking for drinks, telling you they heard a noise, and going to the bathroom for the twentieth time. This routine may be accompanied by arguing and screaming, which only serve to ensure that everyone will stay awake to watch the late movie together.

Your work days are long enough as it is! With a little thought, this kind of bad end to your evenings can be avoided. Many of our Start behavior tactics can be used for bedtime. Put these strategies together and you have the simple and wonderfully helpful Basic Bedtime Method (two-to-four-year-olds will need a little extra help).

The Basic Bedtime Method

Before you can do anything else, you must set a bedtime for the kids and *stick to it*. The bedtime may vary, of course, depending on whether it's a school night or a weekend, or whether it's during the school year or summertime. But exceptions to the rule should be rare. Otherwise, every night bedtime is open for negotiation, which can lead to testing and manipulation, which in turn can lead to no one feeling like sleeping.

Let's assume that you have a nine-year-old daughter, and you decide that 9:00 will be the time for her to go to bed on a school night. The Basic Bedtime method goes like this. At 8:30 you set a timer for 30 minutes and tell the child that it's time to get ready for bed. This means that the youngster must do everything required to prepare for bed—on her own—and then report to you. She must get her pajamas on, brush her teeth, take a shower or bath and do whatever else you require. Be sure to make the bedtime preparation list perfectly clear. If your child is only two or three or four, you'll have to help her get ready, but the same rewards and consequences will apply.

When the child has completed all the necessary tasks, she reports to you. You make sure she accomplished everything she had to and then praise the child for her efforts. Now comes the reward. Whatever time is left between 8:30 and 9:00 is time for just the two of you. This is a great time to share a Bible story or devotion and pray with your child. It is also a great time to just simply sit and talk about the day. Kids love this kind of one-on-one time with a parent. Make sure you stay in the bedroom and don't do anything overly exciting or energetic.

Quik Tip...

The Basic Bedtime Method will save you lots of aggravation in the evenings. The first requirement is that you pick a bedtime—and stick to it! Bedtime cannot be renegotiated every single night.

This special time serves three purposes. First, it is an immediate reinforcer for the child's independently doing a good job of getting ready for bed. Second, the remaining minutes till 9:00 are a good opportunity to pass on your faith and spend a little quiet time together. With all of us so busy these days, this kind of time is not easy to come by. And finally, these moments with you help the kids relax and get in the mood—physically and mentally—for going to sleep. You certainly wouldn't want the children running around wildly right before they're supposed to hit the sack.

If you have trouble coming up with an inventory of all that needs to be done for the kids to get ready for bed, just think of all the things the children usually tell you *they haven't done* after they are *in bed*, and you'll have the list right away.

"I'm hungry."
"I'm scared."
"I need a drink."
"I have to go to the bathroom."
"These pajamas itch."
"There's a burglar in the basement."
"The dog's still outside."

Etc., etc., etc. Every item on the list should be taken care of or addressed before bedtime, even if the item isn't perfectly rational.

One caution here. Don't lie down on the bed. This has nothing to do with anything Freudian. It just so happens that there is a biological law that says: If you are over twenty-five years of age, and it's past 8:00 in the evening, and you spend more than three minutes in a horizontal position, you're gone! You'll be out like a light. And the kids will love it. They'll enjoy the comfort and novelty of having you sleeping next to them, but they will also quickly get dependent on this arrangement and start expecting — or demanding — the same thing every night.

And now, on to the grand finale of the Basic Bedtime Method. When 9:00 rolls around, tuck the child in, kiss her goodnight and leave the room. You have just had a nice time with your youngster and your parenting job is done for the day.

Right? Perhaps not. At this point some parents say, "How naive you are; the kid is right behind me!" or "If I go down to the kitchen, she's sure to show up in less than three minutes wanting something." What if your daughter won't stay in bed after 9:00?

Getting Out of Bed

Some kids just can't seem to stay in bed after you tuck them in. You put them down and they get up. While you try to go about your business, they are always coming up with some new reason for getting out of bed.

When my son was eighteen months old, he climbed out of his crib for the first time. My wife and I were sitting in the living room of our two flat, relaxing and thinking the day was over, when in walked this cute little kid, grinning from ear to ear, proud as punch that he had singlehandedly escaped from his crib for the first time in his life. As young parents, we interpreted this event as the end of the known world. We had visions of our little guy getting up at 3:00 in the morning, calling his friends on the phone, roasting marshmallows on the gas stove, or worse.

In desperation—and forgetting temporarily that I was supposed to

CAUTION

Never forget one very important fact: If a child won't stay in bed at bedtime, the longer he is up and the farther away he gets from his bedroom, the more reinforcement he will get from that activity. Your job? Cut him off at the pass.

be a clinical child psychologist—I found some scrap lumber and some bailing twine and built the sides of his crib up about a foot higher all the way around. The result was quite a contraption, and I wasn't sure it would work.

It didn't. On the third night our boy figured out a way to scale even these new heights and once again escape. So we had to come up with a new plan. Talking to an eighteen-month-old would have been useless. Not only that, by now our son considered getting out of his crib as a kind of exciting challenge. So my wife and I decided that our only choice was to train him some way to remain in bed—or at least in his bedroom.

We put a chair in the door to his room, and after all the bedtime prep was done, one of us (we took turns) just sat in the chair, facing into the hallway. We left the side of his crib down, because putting it up was now useless. We said nothing after bedtime. If our son got out of bed, we put him back in bed. We repeated this procedure and did our best to stay calm. Sometimes we'd give up putting him back in bed, and he'd just fall asleep on the floor. Then we'd cover him and leave, because if we tried to pick him up he'd wake up.

After a week or two, he started staying in his bed and going to sleep. What a relief! I think he actually found our nearby presence comforting, even though we weren't talking to him. In another week or so, we no longer had to sit in the doorway. A couple of months later, our little lad graduated to a junior bed and we never had any more problems.

The strategy for handling kids' getting out of bed is based on a basic psychological principle: *If a child gets out of bed after bedtime, the longer he is out of bed and the longer he stays up, the more reinforcement he gets for this behavior.* And the more he will want to keep getting out of bed in the future. The essential conclusion, therefore, is that you have to "cut him off at the pass"—the doorway to the room. This tactic is certainly no fun for mom or dad, but bedtime is no time for wishful thinking. Bedtime is also no time for ridiculous conversations with little kids about why they should stay in bed.

Just park yourself in a chair in the doorway—facing away from the child. Bring a good book if you want. Don't talk no matter what the youngster says. If he gets out of bed and comes to you, take him gently by the arm or pick him up and put him back.

If you have a child who is over five or six, you might be able to use charting to encourage the youngster to stay in bed. There is a unique problem, though, when it comes to charting bedtime. In general, rewards and punishments are most effective when they are given out immediately. If you are using charting with bedtime, however, you cannot tell the child right away how he did, because if he does really well, he won't be awake. Therefore, there will be a long delay—till the next morning—before he finds out how you rated him, and you may find that this delay reduces the effectiveness of the charting procedure. In spite of this complication, this particular Start behavior strategy may still be worth a try.

Nighttime Waking

Many children go through periods when they wake up at night and present themselves at your bedside with some kind of vague request for assistance. Some kids may get out of bed a dozen or more times per night, while others will just make a little noise and then go back to sleep.

Nighttime problems are among the hardest to handle, because in the middle of the night most parents aren't quite in their right minds—and neither are their kids. It can also be very aggravating to be awakened from a sound sleep, and sleep deprivation itself can have a very bad effect on your next day at work. Handling nighttime problems incorrectly can make matters worse very rapidly, and the child's waking can quickly become more frequent and more traumatic for everybody.

When our daughter was seven, she went through a phase in which she would appear at our bedside in the middle of the night. When we would ask what the problem was, she would say something nonsensical, such as "The elephant ran away." Of course, at 2:00 you're not thinking clearly either, so we would respond with something equally ridiculous, such as "Well, where did he go?" These strange episodes went on for several months until we worked out the nighttime waking procedure that I'm about to describe.

Below are a number of steps that have proved to be effective in responding to nighttime episodes. When these steps are carried out consistently and calmly, most kids will get back to sleeping through the night in a few weeks. Remember: If ever there was a time for our No-Talking and No-Emotion rules, it's in the middle of the night!

1. Accept some periodic waking as normal

Treat periodic nighttime waking as a temporary stage. This way of thinking will help you be less upset. Obviously, if the problem has been going on for the last four years, it's not a temporary "stage." Talk to your pediatrician about the problem.

2. No Talking and No Emotion

These calming rules apply doubly for nighttime, because talking and emotion—especially anger—wake everyone up. Have you ever tried to sleep when you're furious? You can't; your body and mind will simply not let you. In the middle of the night, even asking a child what's wrong is usually pointless, because the child is groggy, not in her right mind and can't tell you much. The No Talking and No Emotion rules apply also to bad dreams. If necessary, discuss the nightmares the next day. Chances are the child will have forgotten the whole incident.

3. Assume the child may have to go to the bathroom

Your son appears at your bedside at 2:30 a.m., mumbling something incoherent. Somebody is probably going to have to get up. This is an interesting situation, because this scene is one in which certain people—especially the fathers—could win Academy Awards for sleeping performances. Dad's snoring deepens and the covers go over his head. If there are two of you living in the house, agree to take turns.

Assume the child has to go to the bathroom—even if he's mumbling about a bad dream or something else. Even though they don't or can't say it, many kids are awakened by the urge to go to the bathroom. But they're so groggy in the middle of the night that they aren't sure what the feeling is and they can't verbalize the physical sensation well. So try steering or carrying them to the toilet and see what happens. Don't ask the youngster if he has to go, unless you know from past experience he is capable of giving you an accurate answer.

4. Be gentle and quiet

Handle and guide the children softly as you stagger through the dark. Don't grab them or push them around, and don't say anything. Bite your tongue, even though you may be irritated that they woke you up. Remember that you want the kids to remain sleepy.

5. No lights!

Lights wake parents and children up very quickly, which then makes it hard to go back to sleep. Your eyes should be dark-adapted in the middle of the night, so just totter around without turning anything on.

> **Quik Tip...**
>
> If a child appears at your bedside in the middle of the night, assume the child has to go to the bathroom. Try steering or carrying him to the toilet and see what happens. Be very gentle and very quiet—and be sure to turn on no lights, which wake everybody up.

6. Don't go to the child's room unless you have to

When do you have to go to the child's room during the night? If she is really upset or won't quiet down, you'd better check things out. On the other hand, many kids will make some noise, fuss around for a while and then go back to sleep. Give them a chance to do so.

7. Don't let the child sleep with you on a regular basis

Sleeping together can become a habit that's hard to break later on. Unfortunately, letting the child crawl in bed with you is the easiest way to quiet him down right at the time. In addition, staying in bed certainly is tempting, but you will pay for these moments of weakness in two ways. First, you will pay right away if the child really has to go to the bathroom, because he will remain squirmy. Second, you will pay later on when you cannot get the lad to return to his room without having a tantrum.

One semi-exception to this rule is this: If there's a terrible storm going on outside, complete with thunder and lightning, let the kids sleep on the floor next to your bed with sleeping bags and pillows. They'll do it, and they'll appreciate the psychological comfort. We had this deal with our kids when they were little. During any stormy night, within forty-five seconds of the first thunderous bang outside, our bedroom door would open and two small forms would appear. Each had a sleeping bag in one hand and a pillow in the other. It was cute. Without saying a word, the kids would plop down on the floor and immediately go back to sleep, suddenly oblivious to the storm. That's what parents are for.

Nocturnal Narratives

Now, using our seven nighttime steps, let's see if we can persuade a few little tykes to go back to bed—and back to sleep.

Josh, age 9

Josh has been sleeping regularly through the night. Tuesday night, however, he watches a rather scary movie on TV. At 2:45 a.m. you hear a few short, anxious and disconnected sentences.

Waiting for a few minutes to see if he'll awaken or get up, you don't go to his room. After a few minutes he goes back to sleep and is peaceful for the rest of the night.

Rachel, age 6

Rachel has been restless in bed for a few consecutive nights, but she hasn't gotten up. Thursday night, however, she appears at your bedside, shakes you by the arm and says she's scared.

You say nothing, get up, put your arm gently around her shoulder, and steer her to the bathroom. You have her sit on the toilet for awhile, with no lights turned on. Rachel did have to go to the bathroom. When she's finished, you guide your daughter gently back to bed, tuck her in and give her a kiss. You wait for a second by her door, see that she's falling asleep, and after she's quiet for a few minutes, you go back to bed.

Jim, age 4

Jim has been getting up several times a night. He won't go back to bed by himself and starts making a fuss if you tell him to. You can't tell if he's frightened or if it's something else. If you take him to his room, he cries or starts yelling when you try to leave. He says he wants to sleep with you. You know he's not sick, because he was just checked by your pediatrician.

This situation is more difficult, obviously, than the first two examples. You don't want Jim to wake everyone in the house, but you don't like the idea of giving in to his testing either. What should you do?

When Jim appears at your bedside, you escort him to the bathroom first—no lights, no talking. He does need to urinate. Then you take him back to his room, put him in bed and tuck him in. Now you know he'll probably cry if you try to leave, so before he gets a chance to even get upset, you get a chair, park yourself by the bed and wait till he goes back to sleep. If you've done the main things right—such as no lights and no arguing—your son should still be somewhat sleepy. Though this routine is not fun, you soon find that the strategy is working. Jim is going right back to sleep.

With some kids this procedure must be repeated several times a night for several weeks before the child starts sleeping through. So brace yourself. Of all the families I've seen in my practice, the record for the most times getting up in one night is seventeen! This case involved a little three-year-old girl, and we got her to sleep through the night in two months.

If you think you'll have to sit by the bed after tucking your youngster back in during the night, get your chair ready beforehand. Then, after a week or so of using this procedure, gradually start positioning the chair further from the bed. Use each new chair position for three or four days. Eventually, you will wind up sitting just outside the door where the child can't see you. If he asks if you're still there, make some noise like sniffing or moving around, but try not to talk. Soon after that, you shouldn't have to even sit in the chair.

Kendra, age 8

Kendra sleeps almost all the way through the night, but she likes to get up at 5:30 a.m. and come to see you, ready to start her day. You've told her to go back to bed, but she won't.

There are several things you can try in this situation. First, consider adjusting Kendra's bedtime back an hour, say from 8:00 to 9:00; she may not need that much sleep. Use the Basic Bedtime Method. Second, make sure her room isn't getting too much sunlight too early — early light wakes many kids up. Get some room-darkening shades or even consider putting a blanket over the window.

Third, you can also try the procedure from the third example. At 5:30 a.m. put Kendra on the toilet, escort her back to bed and then see if she'll go back to sleep. If the room is darker and she's gone to bed later, this tactic may do the trick.

If it's obvious that your daughter won't go back to sleep, however, you will next try to train her to play in her room instead of waking you. How do you accomplish this supine-yet-Herculean feat? Consider a combination of charting and the 1-2-3. Make a chart, using stars, stickers or numbers, that will keep a record of how well Kendra does in the morning *(1) playing by herself* and *(2) not waking anyone.* Give Kendra her score on the chart and praise her for a good job (immediately!) when you get up.

If Kendra forgets and comes to you at 5:30, say calmly, "Go back to bed, that's 1." Going back to bed at this point is a Start behavior that takes less than two minutes. If the little girl argues or doesn't go, you may count her out, and you may have to escort her back to her room. No extra talking and no emotion. By this time you will be aggravated and fully awake, but after a few days — if Kendra knows you mean business — you may be able to count, go back to sleep and have Kendra go off and play by herself until you get up later on, rested and refreshed.

Don't forget that physical pain can also wake kids up at night, so if your child hasn't had a physical lately and she starts waking, it might be a good idea to have her checked out. In the meantime, use the procedures described here.

Bedtime Questions

What if it's bedtime and the child is not ready for bed?

You can put him in bed with his clothes on. Take off his shoes so he's more comfortable. If he's just a little tyke (2 or 3), *you* put his pajamas on. And remember, don't get caught up in the tempting alternative of lecturing the child about what he should have done. It's late, you're tired, he's tired and it's all too easy to slip up by getting upset.

Is it true that floor fans can help some kids sleep?

Yes. Believe it or not, floor fans do help some children go to sleep and stay asleep. Floor fans produce what is sometimes called "white noise," which is simply a monotonous, repetitive sound that is not disturbing, but may, on the contrary, be calming and soothing. White noise, for example, tends to cover other night noises that may keep kids awake, such as a door closing, a car going by, a toilet flushing, a TV, etc.

When using a floor fan, remember that it's the noise you're looking for, not the wind, though in the summer the air circulation can also help the kids sleep. White noise also makes it easier for you to sneak out of your little one's room at 3:00, after you've gotten up with her for the second time!

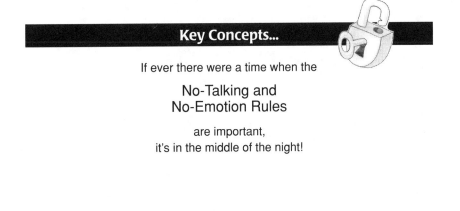

Key Concepts...

If ever there were a time when the

No-Talking and
No-Emotion Rules

are important,
it's in the middle of the night!

Questions for Christian Practice

1. Read Job 35:10, Psalm 42:8, and Acts 16:25. What feelings do these writers possess in the evenings? Can your family sing for joy during your evening routine?

2. What is your current bedtime routine? Can it be improved?

3. Construct an ideal bedtime routine for your family. How will you begin to implement this new plan?

4. What ideas in the sections Getting Out of Bed and Nighttime Waking could you use to help with your child?

5. Do you think a floor fan or white noise machine could help your youngster sleep better?

19
The Family Meeting

If it is possible, as far as it depends on you, live at peace with everyone.

Romans 12:18

The Bible encourages us to live at peace with one another. This can be very challenging for families. A busy calendar, financial pressures and sibling rivalry all create stress that makes family peace and harmony difficult. Parents can facilitate the presence of peace in their family by gradually moving toward a more democratic style of leadership. When your children are small, you, the parent, should be the boss at home. Your parenting should be a kind of benevolent dictatorship, where you make most of the decisions, you are the judge and jury, and you are gentle and kind. Your children will not decide each day what they have for dinner, when they go to bed or whether or not they show up for preschool in the morning.

The reason for this benevolent dictatorship arrangement is two-fold. First, the Bible clearly places the parents in charge of the family. Secondly, you know better than your small kids what is good for them, and you have a right—and a duty—to impose your wishes on the youngsters—even if they don't like it sometimes.

Obviously, counting is a tactic that doesn't give the kids much say in the discipline. That's the way it should be for the welfare of the children as well as the parents. You decide what is Stop behavior and you punish it with a brief time out, but you do so in a way that is fair, calm and not emotionally or physically abusive. Charting and other Start behavior tactics are often friendlier than counting, but these strategies are still largely designed and applied by the grownups in the house.

As your little ones get bigger and bigger, however, the deal should slowly change. By the time your children are late teens, the household should be almost—but not quite—a democracy. Almost a democracy means that these adolescents have a lot more to say about the rules policies that affect them. This becomes possible because over the years you have been teaching and training them in righteousness and giving them more and more independence. Ultimately, your children are responsible to God for their life, and more and more you must let them make their own decisions. Ideally, for example, teens should be making their own decisions about homework, bedtime, choice of friends, clothes and—to a large extent—diet. Gradually encouraging children's growing autonomy is one of a parent's most important challenges.

So how do you foster your kids' spiritual growth and independence? How do you help them make more of their decisions and more of their own mistakes? As we'll see a little later, avoiding what we call overparenting is one critical factor. Another way to encourage your children's spiritual growth and their right to self-determination is the family meeting.

The Board of Directors

The family meeting for a Christian family is a great time for the family to sit down in an organized fashion to experience family worship and to discuss some of the problems of living together. In the New Testament we find this verse: "A new command I give you: Love one another. As I have loved you, so you must love one another" (John 13:34). Keeping this command with the stress of life and sibling rivalry can be very difficult. The family meeting can go a long way toward promoting love between family members. A good time to start family meetings is when the kids are in elementary school. Don't try family meetings when the children are three or four years old, that's a good way to go insane inside of twenty-five minutes.

There are several reasons why a family meeting is a good idea. Life can get so busy that we can forget about our responsibility to nurture the faith of our children. Regularly scheduled family meetings can provide an avenue to nurture your kids' faith. Family meetings can also help move your children toward more autonomous living. As the kids get older it is more appropriate that they have a bigger voice regarding issues that affect them. Some of these issues include chores, phone use, vacations, allowances, discipline and—last but not least—schedules! Most families are busy and going over the weekly practices, games, and events can keep a family more organized. In addition, kids will often cooperate better with a decision or policy when they have had a say in the development of that idea. Finally, children need the experience of family negotiation. This will benefit them greatly when they have their own marriage and their own family to lead.

So the family meeting is a good way to nurture faith, go over schedules and discuss such communal matters as laundry, allowances, bedtimes, renting movies, vacations, food, sibling rivalry, etc. When it comes to dealing with issues the meeting is democratic, but mom and dad still have the final say about unresolved problems.

The family meetings can take place as often as you wish; once every week or two is ideal. You can also call special meetings whenever a unique or urgent problem comes up. And—believe it or not—your kids can request a meeting themselves.

How to Run the Family Meeting

A Christian family may consider dividing the meeting into two parts. The first would be a designated time for family worship. The second part would be devoted to scheduling and other family issues.

In the Christian community there are many different faith traditions, but most share the common points that we will discuss. Feel free to adapt the family worship time to fit your particular tradition. First, most families would include in their meeting some form of prayer. This may include prayers that are read or said from memory. Others might include more spontaneous praying.

Let me suggest a few ways of praying during a family meeting.

Allow a family member to share a prayer request of hers. Then assign that request to another family member. Do this for all family members and then have prayer time together. What a great experience to hear your family praying for one another!

Another great way to use prayer time is to allow family members to share requests, and then you as the parent pray for each member by name. In addition, be sure to include prayers for situations outside your family. This will help your children begin thinking more of the needs of others.

Another family worship idea that most parents would want to include is some form of Bible reading. Develop a plan for regular readings. Your church may also have some suggestions for a systematic reading of God's Word. Other ideas for family meeting worship might include a time for Scripture memory or music, sharing a verse for the week, or the identification of an inspirational quote.

The second part of the Christian family meeting deals more with issues involved in living together. The format for this section is very simple and the guidelines we'll present are only one of many possible ways this can be done. Mom or dad (not both at the same time) is usually the chairperson and has the responsibility for keeping order and for keeping people on task. Older children can take a try at running the meeting themselves from time to time if you think they can handle the job. The chairperson sees to it that the agenda is followed and that each person gets a chance to speak without being interrupted.

What is the agenda? It's very simple. Each person in the family brings to the meeting a problem that he or she wants resolved. Then, with each issue, the chairperson guides the group through the following steps:

1. One person describes the problem she wants resolved.
2. Every other person gives his or her thoughts and feelings about that problem.
3. The floor is opened to proposals for solutions; anyone can speak, but one at a time.
4. A solution to be tried is agreed upon. This final idea may combine aspects of the suggestions from different people. If there are disagreements, mom and dad have the final say.

5. The agreed-upon solution is written down on a piece of paper that is then posted on the refrigerator. Or the solution can be written in a Family Meeting Journal, notebook or computer.

6. The next person brings up his problem, and steps 2-5 are repeated.

Most solutions are considered experimental in the beginning, especially if the plan is complex and differences of opinion about it are large. If the proposed resolution doesn't work too well, that idea can always be reviewed at the next family meeting. Although proposals should be concrete, specific and practical, don't be afraid to make them flexible and imaginative! (See "The Case of the Disappearing Soda" below.)

Sitting through this part of the family meeting is not easy. These sessions are not all warm, fuzzy experiences! In fact, family meetings can be downright obnoxious on occasion. However, the family worship time will often help set the stage for a better get together. Still, it's a good idea to keep the sessions under an hour so you don't go crazy. Sometimes our kids would grumble before family meetings, but once we got going they usually participated actively.

Many parents agree that the family meeting is, paradoxically, *one of the most aggravating and one of the most effective things* you can do with your children. If you can get through the process, people in the family do have a greater tendency to follow through with the agreed-upon solutions. It's also nice that everyone has a chance to speak out and to learn some negotiation skills.

Problems and Solutions: Two Examples

1. The Case of the Disappearing Soda

When she was nine, my daughter brought this weighty issue to our bimonthly family meeting. The girl explained that Mom or Dad usually bought an eight-pack of soda pop, and there were four people in the family. The problem was that she wasn't getting her two bottles. There was never any left! We all listened to our daughter's description of the problem, then brother, Mom and Dad all threw in their opinions.

After some jockeying around we found a solution. When the eight-pack of pop entered the house, all eight bottles would be initialed with a felt marker: two for Mom, two for Dad, two for sister and two for brother. If you drank your two bottles, you were done having pop until the next eight-pack arrived. If you still wanted more pop at some time after you had consumed your own two bottles, you followed a specific procedure. First, you had to check the eight-pack to see if there were any full bottles left and, if there were, whose initials were on the bottles. If there was a full one, you could purchase it for fifty cents from the person who "owned" it. If the person declined to sell, however, no testing and manipulation was allowed.

This agreement was posted on the refrigerator and it worked like a charm.

2. The Incredible Case of the Summer Bedtimes

My son brought this issue to one of our family meetings when he was about eleven. Apparently he and his sister had conspired before the meeting to suggest that summer bedtime should be different from bedtime during the school year. In fact, the kids didn't think they should have a specific bedtime at all during the summer, since they could sleep the next day.

The unbelievable part of this case is that my wife and I agreed to the kids' proposal! Although this idea made us somewhat uneasy, we agreed to try the plan on one condition: If we parents went to bed before the kids did, the kids would have to be amazingly quiet and could not wake us up. Otherwise the deal would be changed.

After a few nights of trial and error, the deal was changed at another meeting because the kids were waking us up. The new deal, which worked well, was this: If the kids woke us up, they had to go to bed immediately.

Points to Remember...

1. Christian family meetings are useful in nurturing the faith of children.

2. Going over the family's schedule during family meetings can help keep a family more organized.

3. Family meetings are very useful in resolving family issues, but can be aggravating and difficult to sit through.

4. Keep family meetings short and expect some resistance from your children.

Questions for Christian Practice

1. Read James 1:19, Proverbs 18:13 and Ephesians 4:29. How can these verses be applied to running a Family Meeting?

2. What concerns do you have about beginning family meetings?

3. What are some possible conflicts in your family that could be addressed in a family meeting?

4. Write an agenda for your first family meeting. Include time, place and goals.

5. Once decisions are made, how will you ensure follow-through?

20
When Do You Talk?

...a time to tear and a time to mend, a time to be silent and a time to speak...
Ecclesiastes 3:7

The No-Talking and No-Emotion rules do not mean that you never should talk to your kids about their troublesome behavior. But there are good times to talk and explain and bad times to talk and explain. The writer of Ecclesiastes had it right; there is a time to be silent and a time to speak. The trick is knowing when to speak and when to be silent. In Proverbs we find, "a word aptly spoken is like apples of gold in settings of silver" (Proverbs 25:11).

Knowing the best time to talk to your children about their behavior can bring better results. *Generally the time when a rule is being enforced is a bad time.* Why? Because this brief period of time is not a good learning moment for most kids. You are likely to be irritated with your child. Chances are she is mad at you, too. She may at the same time feel anxious, guilty and defensive about what just happened.

Talking during this time of unpleasant emotional arousal produces two problems. First, talking at this point encourages arguing. There are lots of children who do not relish the idea of humiliating themselves by admitting that you—and all your reasons—are correct, while their behavior was absolutely wrong. To save face, therefore, the youngsters may feel obligated to disagree with you. And if you get into an argument over what just happened, you have accomplished nothing.

Second, it is very likely that all your ideas about your child's behavior *are* correct. Parents are not stupid and they do not go around saying dumb things to their children most of the time. Even though your ideas are good, your child is not openminded during discipline episodes. At that moment she doesn't want to hear what you have to say, and your attempts to explain only aggravate her more. This irritation motivates your daughter to contradict what you are saying—even if only in her mind. So what have you accomplished? You have given your little one an opportunity to throw your good ideas into the trash.

When should you talk about problems? You should explain something right away if a child's problem behavior is new, unusual or dangerous. Your child decides to use your couch as a trampoline, for instance. This behavior is new and unusual, and you also feel it's dangerous. So you explain to your son that he can't jump on the couch because he might hurt himself or hurt the furniture. Using a new swear word or hitting someone else are also examples of times when you would explain to your child why he can't do something. Remember to keep your explanations short and to the point. Look at your child's facial expressions; you can usually tell when he is tuning you out. If possible, wrap the conversation up at that point.

Ask a Few Questions First

Instead of jumping in and anxiously explaining right away, when time permits many parents use a kind of questioning technique to help kids think a problem through. The questions might be something like these:

> What would happen if you did that?
> Why is this a good thing to do?
> How did you feel when I said that to you?
> Why do you think I want you to do your homework?
> Why is it bad to push someone?
> Why does your teacher ask you to be quiet?

Questioning forces the child to think an issue through himself, rather than passively listening to a brilliant parental lecture. This required mental activity, in the presence of a non-angry adult, often helps kids remember the lesson a little better. Questions followed by brief adult explanations can be an effective strategy for teaching children how to behave.

Whether you decide at any one point to explain or to question, keep in mind that short, calm talking sessions are always better than long, angry lectures.

Insight Plus Practice

What if a problem behavior is not new, unusual or dangerous, but instead is minor, but also repetitious and irritating? In spite of your explanations, for example, your seven-year-old daughter still whines occasionally when she doesn't get her way, and she often forgets to pick up after herself. When she whines, you have told her to use her "big girl voice." When she leaves toys and books lying around, you have explained that you are not the maid.

What's the problem? The problem is she's just a kid! It takes children a while to learn how to avoid Stop behavior and how to successfully complete certain Start behaviors. So give your youngsters a break—be patient and realistic.

Adults often forget that children's mastery of behavioral skills depends not only on insight (explanation) but also on practice (repetition). You certainly didn't master the art of driving a car by simply reading about it in a book. You also did not become a competent driver simply because your driving instructor told you where the ignition, steering wheel, gas pedal and brake pedal were. Although those concepts were useful bits of knowledge, you still had to go out and practice, practice, practice. And you had to practice under different conditions. You had to drive in good and bad weather, with a pleasant or angry or worried adult, and at times when you were in a good mood or in a bad mood.

CAUTION

It's not reasonable or fair for you to expect your children to behave properly just because you've explained something once to them. Remember that good behavior requires practice, practice, practice! You did not learn how to drive a car by reading a book.

The same is true of your children. Don't ever underestimate how much *behavioral rehearsal* is required before kids can master skills such as talking in a normal voice (when frustrated) and remembering to pick up after yourself (when you'd much rather run out and play with a friend).

If you want to give your child a little talk from time to time about good and bad behavior, by all means do so. But try not to talk right at the time a rule is being enforced. And keep in mind that kids are not little adults; you don't train them to behave just by pouring information into their heads. In addition to our explanations, we adults often forget that our youngsters have many other ways of learning good and bad behavior:

- Parental modeling
- Behavior modeling by other children, including siblings
- Books, television and music
- Praise that follows good behavior
- Counting that follows obnoxious behavior
- Adults' comments regarding the behavior of other people, including children and adults
- Behavioral experimentation: trying out something and seeing what happens
- And many more...

When discipline or conflict is not involved, of course, talk as much as you want to. In fact, as Christians we are commanded to talk about and teach God's ways to our children. "Teach them (God's laws and commands) to your children, talking about them when you sit at home and when you walk along the road, when you lie down and when you get up" (Deuteronomy 11:19). One of the things most parents love about parenting is watching their children's young minds think, grow, learn and change. Small children are learning machines, and it's fascinating to be a part of—and to encourage—that process.

Points to Remember...

1. The time when discipline is being enforced is usually not a good time to explain, because a child is not openminded.

2. Do explain right away if a problem is new, unusual or dangerous.

3. Before you talk, ask your child some thought-provoking questions.

4. Remember that kids learn good behavior in many different ways!

Questions for Christian Practice

1. Read Proverbs 15:2, Proverbs 15:23, James 1:26, and Ephesians 4:29. How can you apply these verses to the issue of how and when you talk to your children?

2. Describe a time when you tried to explain or talk too much during discipline.

3. When dealing with misbehavior, do you think your child will learn more from you asking questions or giving a lecture? Why?

4. Are you guilty of expecting your child to master behavioral skills without enough practice? How can remembering that children need lots of practice help you be a better parent?

5. What are some ways you teach God's law to your children?

Part V

Strengthening Your Relationship

21
Your Child's Self-Esteem

And Jesus grew in wisdom, and stature, and in favor with God and men.

Luke 2:52

Y ou've been working hard and at this point in the *1-2-3 Magic for Christian Parents* program you've accomplished a lot. You've taken the first two giant parenting steps. Your home is a more peaceful and enjoyable place in which to live.

Step 1 was learning how to control difficult (Stop) behavior. Now you routinely and calmly count obnoxious behavior. And the kids cease and desist, amazingly, almost all the time at 1 or 2. You certainly don't miss that whining at all! Sibling rivalry you have accepted as a fact of life, but the amount of teasing and fighting has dropped dramatically since you've instituted the four basic rules for managing the kids' battles. Sure, sometimes you get a little too excited and start chattering some, but you're able to catch yourself and quiet down.

In parenting Step 2, you began using the strategies for encouraging good (Start) behavior. This task was easier because, after you had counted for a while, the kids understood that when you said something, you meant business. But you also found out that Start behavior meant more motivation was required for the kids and more motivation was also required of you! Nevertheless, you established your routines for daily tasks like bedtime, eating meals, homework and getting up and out in the morning. Now the kids are happily doing a lot more on their own and you are not nagging and arguing anymore. The house is not filled with the screaming and crying that before were symptomatic of all those aggravating—and depressing—power struggles. Incredibly, your children are also better at picking up after themselves; the place is a lot neater!

In short, your kids are better behaved, happier and they listen. You are able to enjoy their energy, their enthusiasm and their curiosity. You have discovered that your children are cute, engaging and have a keen sense of humor. And as a result of all this, you like yourself much more as a parent.

Well, guess what? It's time to take the third and last step up the parenting ladder. The third step involves strengthening (and enjoying) your relationship with your child. This last step also includes—inevitably—taking a realistic look at the issue of your youngster's self-esteem.

Your Relationship and Your Child's Self-Esteem

Your relationship with your child and your child's self-esteem are closely intertwined. Just about anything you do to improve your relationship will also improve your child's self-esteem. But you'll also be happy to know that everything you've done so far, in parenting steps 1 (controlling Stop behavior) and 2 (encouraging Start behavior), has also done a lot to increase the positive self-regard of your son or daughter. To understand this, we need to take a look at what self-esteem is really all about (for further information, see our companion volume, *Self-Esteem Revolutions in Children*).

Everyone has worth and value because everyone was created by God. "I praise you because I am fearfully and wonderfully made, your works are wonderful, I know that full well" (Psalm 139:14). In this verse the psalmist recognizes his value and praises God for this fact. We do indeed have worth that is not tied to our accomplishments because of God's unconditional love for us. This is the beginning for our self-esteem.

However, our self-esteem is also highly affected by our actions. In this sense our self-esteem is a tough, reality-based business. Contrary to what some teach, self-esteem is not a make-the-kids-feel-good-at-all-cost kind of project. If certain qualities are lacking in one's life, positive self-esteem cannot be bestowed instantly in a kind, insightful moment, in a weekend workshop, or in a positive summer camp experience. Self-esteem is based on reality, not gimmicks.

There is a story about a fourth-grade teacher—a very nice, well-meaning lady—who was very concerned about fostering self-esteem in her students. One day during geography, she asked the class a question:

"What is the capitol of Egypt?"

One young man in the back of the room waved his hand
enthusiastically.

"Johnny?" said the teacher.

"Mississippi." Johnny replied confidently.

Temporarily taken aback, but not wanting to injure her young student's developing self-concept, Johnny's teacher quickly recovered and said, "That's the correct answer to another question."

In addition to this statement's almost being a lie, this adult maneuver is an example of a superficial gimmick designed to protect a young boy's self-esteem. The correct response from the teacher should have been: "Wrong."

The issue here is this: *Realistic and positive self-esteem is the by-product of a life well-lived.* Luke gave us a glimpse of a child who lived well when he described Jesus' childhood, "And Jesus grew in wisdom, and stature, and in favor with God and men" (Luke 2:52). This small glimpse into the life of Jesus shows us that a well-lived life is based on more than one area. Several key areas of a life well lived include: social competence (getting along with others, being loved and appreciated), work competence (for kids this largely involves school, but it also involves independent self-management skills), physical competence (physical skills and caring for one's body), and character competence (ability to follow the rules, effort, courage and concern for others). By and large, therefore, whatever you do as a parent to help your child become competent in these areas is going to improve your child's self-esteem.

Our Three Parenting Steps and Your Child's Self-Esteem

When you began with our first parenting step, counting obnoxious behavior, you were helping your child with her self-esteem in a very important and basic way. No one, child or adult, is going to get along very well with others if she is continually arguing, whining (adults whine too!), teasing, yelling or putting others down. Obnoxious people have a hard time making and keeping friends. Learning self-control and not doing what you shouldn't is also a big part of the last self-esteem element—character.

Second, when you started systematically encouraging positive (Start) behavior, you were also helping your child with his self-esteem, because Start behavior involves learning how to independently manage your life. Kids who know how to get out of the house in the morning, complete their homework, feed the dog and get to bed—on their own—naturally feel better about themselves. Independence makes kids proud.

Finally, having a good relationship with your child—and working to strengthen that relationship—is obviously a big part of the social competence element of self-esteem. As your kids get older, they will be required to get along with more and more children as well as with more and more adults. In their relationship with you, your youngsters get their critical first experience about how to get along with somebody else.

There is another very good reason for working on your relationship with your child: Keeping your relationship positive, enjoyable and healthy will make the other two parenting tasks—counting obnoxious behavior and encouraging good behavior—much, much easier.

In the next few chapters we'll discuss some simple but effective ways to improve and build your relationship with your children. Chapter 22 will explain how to avoid a big self-esteem killer: overparenting. In Chapter 23 we'll provide some helpful tips on the issues of praise and affection. Then, in Chapter 24, we'll have a big surprise for you regarding the notion of family togetherness and what to do about it. Chapter 25 will explore the ins and outs of a too-often-forgotten parental task: listening sympathetically to the little ones. In that same chapter, we'll discuss how to integrate listening with counting. Turning that switch from warm to demanding and back—again and again—is no easy task!

Key Concepts...

Healthy self-esteem is based on these elements:

1. The unconditional love of God

2. Good relationships with other people

3. Competence in work and self-management

4. Physical skills and caring for one's body

5. Character: courage, effort, following the rules and concern for others.

Questions for Christian Practice

1. Read Ephesians 4:29-32. How can these verses be applied to how you parent?

2. Describe a self-esteem building moment from your own life?

3. How do you feel your child is doing in each of the 4 areas of competence listed in this chapter (page 201)?

4. What are some specific ways you can help your child develop a more positive self-esteem?

5. Read Romans 5:8. Take a moment and thank God for his unconditional love for us.

22
Overparenting

For each one should carry his own load.
Galatians 6:5

Paul encourages us to "Carry each other's burden, and in this way you will fulfill the law of Christ" (Galatians 6:2). As parents this admonition includes our children. We should help our children with the struggles of life. However, Paul goes on to tell us "For each one should carry his own load" (Galatians 6:5). According to this verse, there are some areas that each of us must shoulder alone.

Children are not excluded. There is a temptation for many parents to be over-involved in their children's lives. This can be frustrating to both the parent and the child. Recently I was in a grocery store standing in front of the dairy case. As I was trying to decide which kind of milk to buy, I noticed a mother with a girl, about nine, pushing a cart and coming around the corner toward me. As they came closer, the mother said anxiously, "Now watch out for that man over there!"

I'm an average-sized adult male of about 180 pounds. There was no way this young lady was not going to see me. Even if she had been traveling at 40 miles per hour, she would still have had plenty of room to stop before crashing into my legs. Mom's comment was an example of what we sometimes call "overparenting." Overparenting refers to *unnecessary* corrective, cautionary or disciplinary comments made by parents to kids. These parental comments can be unnecessary for several reasons:

1. The child already has the skill necessary to manage the situation.
2. Even if the child doesn't have all the necessary skills to manage the situation, it would be preferable for the youngster to learn by direct experience.
3. In addition to 1 or 2, the issue involved is trivial.

The child can manage.

In our dairy case example above, the nine-year-old girl certainly had the ability to (a) see me in her path, (b) appreciate the fact that it would not be good to hit me and (c) stop the cart in time or turn away. The average nine-year old would not need parental direction in this situation. Unfortunately, when she saw her daughter heading toward me, the girl's mother became nervous. Though she may have actually trusted that her daughter would not run into me, this Mom wanted to be doubly sure, so she gave her the unnecessary, cautionary warning.

Here's another common example of a pointless parental adminition: "Now don't drop your ice cream cone!" How many kids want to deliberately throw their tasty treat onto the ground? Not many.

Learning by experience may be better.

When our kids were little and after we moved into our first house, I used to watch the children playing out in the yard. To my dismay, it seemed that about every five minutes an incident would occur which I felt needed my intervention. Then I would rush outside trying to mediate some dispute among the children or otherwise correct the situation. Some days, especially on weekends, I would conduct multiple diplomatic missions.

Then one day my wife pointed out to me an interesting and simple fact. She explained that during all the hours I was away from home every week—which was well over 50 hours—no child had ever been killed, suffered a broken arm or leg, had an eye poked out, or sustained any other serious injury. Not only that, our kids were successfully making friends and in general having a good time playing outdoors.

The point? I was overparenting. In the realm of neighborhood child politics, my supervision and consulting services were not necessary. Though there were times of social conflict, our kids were learning how to handle these new relationships pretty much on their own.

The issue is trivial.

Mike and Jimmy are out in the front yard playing catch with a baseball. Jimmy's Dad is washing the car in the driveway while the neighbor, Mr. Smith, is cutting his grass next door. Mike misses Jimmy's throw and the ball rolls over toward Mr. Smith, who smiles and tosses it back. Dad tells the two boys they will have to go somewhere else or stop playing catch. Should Dad have kept quiet? Yes, he should have.

The issue here was truly unimportant. Dad's oversensitivity motivated him to intervene when he should have said nothing. Let the two lads work it out with Mr. Smith, if that ever becomes necessary. The boys were having innocent, constructive fun, and Mr. Smith probably enjoyed trying out his old pitching arm again!

Anxious Parent, Angry Child

Though the incidents we just described are all sort of trivial, the issue of overparenting itself is not—for two reasons: (1) parents who overparent usually do it repeatedly, and (2) overparenting has predictable, negative effects on children. Kids will have several reactions to unnecessary parental warnings and unnecessary discipline, and none of these responses will be positive. Add these reactions up over time, and you can have a significant negative impact on a child's personality and self-esteem.

> **CAUTION**
>
> Parents who constantly verbalize their worries about their kids to their kids unfortunately accomplish two things, both of them bad: (1) the adults irritate their youngsters and (2) they undermine their children's self-esteem.

The first negative reaction kids have to overparenting is anger. This is what we call the "Anxious Parent, Angry Child" syndrome. *Anxious moms and dads who continually verbalize their worries about their kids to their kids will inevitably irritate the youngsters.* Sometimes, of course, verbalizing a worry or concern is necessary. "Remember to look both ways before crossing the street," said to a four-year old who doesn't have that skill yet, is necessary for the child's safety.

It's the consistent and pointless repetition of worries that aggravates youngsters. Why do kids find this repetition aggravating? In short, because it insults them. The parent's basic message is this: I have to worry about you so much because you're incompetent; there's not much you can do on your own without my supervision and direction. No child likes to be put down, and overparenting is definitely a put-down.

That point leads us to the second negative reaction children have to unnecessary parental interventions: the undermining of the child's confidence. If you grow up constantly hearing your parents' thoughts about how you can't handle this and you can't handle that, you're not going to have a very high opinion of your own abilities. "Now don't get too loud at the party and be sure to take turns and remember to thank Mrs. Johnson and be nice to the other children and..." The message as received: "You're a social imbecile."

Overparenting is the opposite of one of a parent's most fundamental jobs: fostering self-esteem by encouraging independence and autonomy. As they get older, kids must learn to handle more and more on their own. After all, a main goal of most parents is not to have their children living at home for the rest of their lives.

So next time you get the urge to warn or discipline — or even count — a child, ask yourself a few questions. Can my daughter handle this situation on her own? Would it be better in this case for her to learn by direct experience? Is the issue important enough for me to get involved?

Sometimes it's better to keep quiet, cross your fingers, do your best to relax and watch your child learn and mature. Consider the exercise an investment in both your child's self-esteem and in her future.

Points to Remember...

One of your most important tasks as a parent is to foster and encourage your child's growing independence. If you happen to be an unnecessary worrier, think about how many of your worries you should keep to yourself.

Questions for Christian Practice

1. Read Proverbs 9:12 and Proverbs 10:16. What do these verses say about personal responsibility? How can that be applied to parenting?

2. Describe a time when you over-parented.

3. How does your child react to you when you over-parent?

4. How can being over-involved with your child hinder the learning process?

5. In what areas do you tend to over-parent? How can you back away from these situations?

23
Affection and Praise

Love each other with genuine affection, and take delight in honoring each other.
Romans 12:10 (New Living Translation)

In Romans we are encouraged to love and honor others. Children benefit greatly when parents practice these concepts by giving loving affection and honoring praise. Loving affection is a self-esteem builder for kids because it represents a direct confirmation of the young person and it contributes to the social-competence part of the self-esteem equation. Praise is the "I like—or I am proud of—what you are doing" part of parenting. Praise is also a self-esteem builder because it recognizes and reinforces competent behavior in a child.

When it comes to affection and praise, however, parents have a harder job than you might expect. While affection and praise are obvious self-esteem boosts to children as well as great relationship strengtheners, we parents usually do not engage in these types of behavior nearly as often as we should. We mentioned one reason for this deficit in Chapter 13: the "Angry Parents Speak, Happy Ones Keep Quiet" rule. This "rule" refers to the tendency of adults to give feedback to children when the adults are angry, but to keep quiet when the adults are happy with the youngsters' behavior.

Our inherent biological perversity—the fact that we speak more when angry and don't praise or act affectionately unless we really, really feel like it—is one of the big reasons why we asked you first to learn how to control kids' *obnoxious* behavior in parenting Step 1, and later to learn how to encourage kids' *positive* behavior in parenting Step 2. Success at Steps 1 and 2 will make you more inclined to apply the relationship-strengthening parts of the *1-2-3 Magic for Christian Parents* program.

Your success with those two initial tasks will automatically make you *feel* more affectionate toward your kids and also make you *feel* more like giving them positive feedback. That extra motivation is very important because you are human, you are busy and you can't always remember to do everything you're supposed to do.

Quik Tip...

Your success with Step 1, controlling obnoxious behavior, and Step 2, encouraging good behavior, will make you feel more affectionate towards your kids. That's important because it helps you remember to give positive feedback.

But a positive feedback deficit can also result from two other things: (1) how a parent is feeling about life in general and (2) how a parent is feeling toward a child, in general and at any one particular moment. Just because a child does something that is commendable, for example, does not mean that she will be recognized or praised for that action. Let's examine these two issues.

Mom and Dad: How Are *You* Doing?

Research has confirmed what common sense has long suggested: Parents who are unhappy and suffering in their own lives are not going to give a lot of praise and affection to their children. Depressed parents, for example, are known for being detached, isolated and sometimes almost indifferent to their kids. These moms and dads simply do not have a lot of extra positive energy to throw around. And their children know it and feel it.

A parent's energy can also be sapped by long hours in a stressful job that involves a difficult supervisor and impossible challenges. In addition, lots of parental energy can go into worrying about one's own aging parents, concerns about one's own physical health, or exhaustion from a conflict-filled marriage. All these stresses make parents more self-centered and less likely to reward their kids for the good things the little ones do.

The moral of the story, naturally, is that to effectively express the affection and praise that your children can thrive on, as a parent you must take pretty good care of yourself in the first place. You need to see that your needs are being met and that you are not chronically locked into helpless, angry, martyrlike or victim roles.

Maybe it's time to join a healthy small group Bible study. Connecting with other believers for prayer, Bible study and accountability can help meet some of your own needs and help you focus better on life's issues. Perhaps it's time for that physical you've been putting off. Or maybe it's possible that larger tasks confront you. Do you need to seriously reevaluate your job situation and consider either learning to manage your boss better or leaving your company? (Yes, I said learning to manage your boss better!) Or do you need to sit down with your spouse and—in a gentle but firm manner—confront the fact that the two of you are drifting apart and not having any fun together anymore?

Whatever the case, the amount of praise and affection your children receive from you will depend, in large part, on your success in diagnosing and resolving your own problems.

Quik Tip...

If you're not giving the kids the praise and affection they will thrive on, perhaps your life needs a little work. It's very hard to be a good parent if you don't take good care of yourself first!

Your Feelings Toward Your Child

I have seen many parents over the years who are extremely upset or even devastated by the fact that their child has developed a bad reputation with his peers. Their son, for example, may have few or no friends. He may not get invited to birthday parties. He may be teased or bullied on the playground. Teachers do not look forward to getting the boy in their classes. In short, it seems that other people and the world in general are giving the child no positive—but lots of negative—feedback. And most parents today realize that reputations, like first impressions, are hard to change.

The general opinion you have of someone—that person's reputation with you—will have a lot to do with how much positive and negative feedback you give that individual. And for parents, here's the bad news:

Some kids have a bad reputation with their own parents. The parents love these children but they don't like them. Though few parents who are in this position want to admit it, when you don't really like your own child two unfortunate things happen: (1) you come up way short on expressing affection and praise, and (2) you feel terribly guilty.

What's the solution? The answer is our three parenting steps. First, you have to work hard at reasonably and calmly counting these kids, so they don't drive you crazy with their arguing, whining, teasing and tantrums. Then you have to put on your thinking cap and establish your routines for Start behavior, so these kids don't further aggravate you by being late for school, messing up the house, or not getting to bed on time. And finally, you need to pay attention to all the simple but effective relationship-building strategies we're discussing in Part V of this book, which include one-on-one fun, sympathetic listening and avoiding overparenting.

Be patient. Reputations are hard to change. Over a period of time, though, if you keep at the three parenting steps, you will find that you like your children more and that you are feeling more affectionate toward them. You'll also notice that they like you better — and they listen better! — which leads to your praising them more. When that time comes, the kids' reputations with you will have turned around in a positive direction.

In many ways, affection and praise are to kids what water and fertilizer are to plants. Do you really need to teach parents how to express affection and praise their children? For the most part, I don't think so. Sometimes what you do need to do is to point out some of the barriers that are getting in the way of these natural and extremely valuable pieces of the parenting job.

Key Concepts...

If there is a positive reinforcement (affection and praise) deficit in your house, how are you going to address the problem?

Questions for Christian Practice

1. Read Proverbs 16:24, Proverbs 18:21 and Colossians 4:6. How can these verses be applied to a parent's conversations with her child?

2. Rate yourself on a scale from 1 to 10 on how well you are giving affection and praise to your child (1 = Low, 10 = High).

3. List any areas in your life that are negatively affecting your ability to give praise and affection to your child. What steps are you going to take to address these issues?

4. Make a list of specific ways you can praise your children. Set a goal for how many times a day you want to do this.

5. List some problem areas in your child's life that impair your sense of affection for that youngster. What 1-2-3 Magic strategies will you use to address those issues?

24
Real Magic: One-on-One Fun

...God, who richly supplies all things to enjoy.
1 Timothy 6:17 (NASB)

Some people consider God a cosmic killjoy, when in fact, He is just the opposite. God came to bring us the abundant life. A true Christian's character is marked by joy. Sharing the fun and joy of the Lord with others produces tremendous results. Show us any two people who have fun together frequently and we'll show you a good relationship. Just as praise and affection are like water and fertilizer to a child's self-esteem, shared fun provides the same kind of necessary nutrition to a personal relationship. Whether they are young or old, people who have regular fun together like each other — period. For many families these days, however, this much-needed mutual enjoyment gets put on the back burner because of the unfortunate focus on two things: busywork and whole-family activities.

Work, Work, Work

Do you remember how you got married? Most of us started out by dating another person. By and large, that meant fun. Dating was going to the movies, food, endless getting-to-know-you talks, travel, shopping, parties with friends and a whole host of other activities. Of course, there were times that were a little nerve-wracking, like meeting your future in-laws for the first time, but those were minor blips on the radar screen. The whole thing was new, exciting and enjoyable.

Most of us then went on to make what was perhaps one of the most illogical decisions of our entire existence. We reasoned as follows: Think of all the fun we're having now, and we're not even married. We're only together *half* of the time. Once we're married and together *all* the time, our good times will double!

Admit it—that's what you believed. What was illogical about that thought? The irrational part had to do with the fact that getting married is fundamentally a decision to work together. Now we'll plan the wedding, now we'll get jobs, now we'll have a baby, now we'll buy a condo, now we'll decorate the condo and buy furniture. The former fun got all mixed up with cooking, laundry, paying bills, raising kids, visiting in-laws, grocery shopping and millions of other tasks. Gradually you realized your relationship was getting more and more strained, and you looked at your spouse and silently thought: "You're not as much fun as you used to be."

> **Quik Tip...**
>
> To like your kids you must enjoy them regularly. And for them to respond well to your discipline, they must enjoy and like you too. That means only one thing: You'd better find regular time to play with your youngsters!

In the long run, of course, marriage is a mixture of work and good times, and the successful couples are the ones who can find the happy balance between work and play. And since work seems to fill our time so naturally and aggressively, finding that balance really boils down to maintaining sufficient time for shared fun. If you asked me what's more important in a marriage relationship, communication or shared fun, I would answer, "shared fun."

The same is true in your relationship with each of your children. To like the kids you must enjoy them regularly. And for them to respond positively to your discipline well, they must enjoy and like you. Yes, there is work to be done, but it is absolutely critical that you find time to play with your youngsters.

Unfortunately, in the hustle and bustle of everyday existence, many of the daily encounters between parent and child go something like this:

"Time to get up."

"Here's your breakfast. No TV till you're done."

"Got your book bag?"

"You don't have time to play with the dog."

"Come on now, we're in a hurry!"

"Don't forget your coat."

"Love you, goodbye."

"How was your day? Got any homework?"

"Leave your sister alone!"

"You've got to finish your peas if you want your dessert."

"You can go to Bobby's for one hour. I want you back at 8:00 for bed."

"Give me a kiss goodnight. I don't think you brushed your teeth."

How much mutual enjoyment took place on this day? None. The parent saw the child as a bundle of unpleasant tasks, and the child saw the parent as a bundle of unpleasant directions. No relationship will remain healthy when this kind of interaction is the only feeding it gets.

The antidote? Fun.

The Focus on Whole-Family Activities

Brace yourself for some bad news: Family fun today is way overrated. We consistently hear, for example, that eating dinner as a family every night is the sure-fire way of preventing crime, drug abuse, academic underachievement, teenage pregnancy and a bunch of other social evils.

Going out with the whole crew is not all it's cracked up to be for three reasons. The first is sibling rivalry. Mom and Dad are at the beach, for instance, with eight-year-old daughter and six-year-old son. The adults are trying to enjoy the sand, the water and the kids' interaction. But the boy says something smart to his sister, who throws her hotdog at her brother, who laughs as it misses and gets full of sand. Now both kids are screaming at each other and everyone on the beach is looking. This isn't fun.

The second reason fun with the entire family doesn't always work is this: The more people you put together in the same place, the greater the chance for differences of opinion and conflict. At 9:30 a.m. on day two of their family vacation, for example, the Jeffersons are about to leave their motel room, but they have a problem. Mark wants to go to Creature Castle, which he saw advertised on the interstate. Cynthia wants to go to the pool, and she has already put on her suit. Mom wants to have a leisurely cup of coffee in the restaurant next door to the motel. And finally, Dad wants to get his usual start to the day by jogging three miles.

The third reason that family fun is overrated is this: The best parent-child bonding occurs in one-on-one parent-child interactions. When you were dating, you certainly didn't want to be with other people *all the time*, especially if the group included a few of your greatest rivals. Similarly, children really cherish alone time with a mother or father, without the presence of their greatest rivals—their siblings. Watch the kids when they're alone with you. They open up, they talk, they feel free and they kind of blossom. It would be a shame to rarely—or never—experience that with a child because you're so busy thinking everybody should be constantly together.

Play with Your Youngster

It's very important, therefore, to take your kids, one at a time, and regularly do something you both like. It's more peaceful because there's no fighting; in fact, there's no chance of fighting. And coordinating different agendas is no problem because there are only two agendas to coordinate.

The possibilities for shared one-on-one fun are endless. Many parents I've worked with over the years like to take a son or daughter out to dinner on a schoolnight while everyone else stays home and fends for themselves. Going to a movie, going shopping, bike riding or just going out for a drive in the car can also fill the bill. One of the nice things about getting out of the house is that no one can interrupt you. Your kids will also like it if you turn your cell phone off for a while.

One-on-one fun, though, does not have to entail going out nor does it have to involve spending money. Most children love being able to stay up twenty minutes later on a school night, every now and then, to do something special with mom or dad. That something might be reading, just talking or—heaven forbid!—teaching a naïve and inexperienced parent how to play a video game.

Here are some other ideas for one-on-one playtimes:

Finger painting in the bathtub
Baking cookies (yes, boys and girls!)
Going to the park and reading
Playing catch
Jigsaw puzzles, board or card games
Biking, swimming
Window shopping while walking the mall
Planting a child's garden
Giving the dog a bath
Planning and shopping for a meal
Doing a collection together (stamps,
    cards, coins, dolls)
Visiting a museum
Attending a sporting event (including free Little League games!)
Taking cookies to an elderly neighbor
The zoo!

Key Concept...

The best parent-child bonding occurs during one-on-one fun times. Why? For the kids, they have you all to themselves! And for you, there's absolutely no chance for sibling rivalry. Now there's a formula for success!

Shared fun can also come in little bits and pieces during the day. Little bits of fun can be shared and enjoyed when you are talking, listening, expressing affection or telling jokes. In fact, let's redo the dreary parent-child day we experienced earlier and let's put some fun into it:

"Unfortunately, sleepyhead, it's time to get up." Mom rubs child's
    back.
"After you demolish your breakfast, you can watch a little TV."
"Got your two-ton book bag?"
"That dog sure likes you. OK, let's get outta here!"
"You're moving faster than I am this morning!"
"Glad you remembered your coat."
"Love you, goodbye."
"What was the most fun part of your day?"
"Leave your sister alone. That's 1."
"Only three more peas, my dear, and I will provide you with a

huge dose of chocolate cake."

"You can go to Bobby's for one hour till 8:00. Have a good
time."

"Give me a kiss goodnight. Oops, better brush those teeth."

That was much friendlier and more fun. Affection, praise, listening
and a sense of humor all helped. Sure, a little sibling rivalry inevitably
sneaked into the picture, but it was handled crisply by counting.

The moral of this chapter? By all means, do things together with the
entire family, but make sure those times are as enjoyable as possible. If
whole-family activities are usually miserable experiences, put some real
thought, planning and experimentation into ironing out the trouble spots.
But whatever you do about whole-family fun, make sure your days and
weeks include regular, one-on-one fun with each of your children.

Points to Remember...

Of all our relationship-building strategies, by far the
most powerful is one-on-one fun—one parent with one child.

Questions for Christian Practice

1. Read Nehemiah 8:10, John 10:10 and Galatians 5:22. What do
these verses say about fun and joy in life? How can you apply these
verses to your parenting approach?

2. How would your child respond if asked, "How fun are your
parents?"

3. Describe the last fun time you had with your child.

4. What can you do to make whole family activities more enjoyable
for your family?

5. Develop a list of fun activities that you and your child can do
together. Choose one and try it out this week.

25
Active Listening

My dear brothers, take note of this: Everyone should be quick to listen, slow to speak and slow to become angry.

James 1:19

In the New Testament book of James, we are instructed to be quick to listen. This is not always easy to do with children. It takes wisdom, patience and practice. The benefits, however, are worth the effort.

Imagine your ten-year-old son, Tom, comes running in the door after school yelling, "My music teacher's an idiot!" What should you do? You could count—after all the boy is screaming. But think for a second. He is *not* screaming at you, he *is* upset about something and you don't know what it is. Your priority? Give the child some support and find out what happened. His being angry is no crime, and his outburst couldn't be testing and manipulation, because you didn't do anything to frustrate him.

Here is a time for what is often called "active listening." The conversation might go something like this:

Tom: "My music teacher's an idiot!"

Mom: "Tell me what happened."

Tom: "She made me sing in front of the whole stupid class, and only one other kid had to do it. She didn't care, but all my friends were laughing at me!"

Mom: "What did she make you sing?"

223

Tom: "I don't know, some jerk hymn or something."

Mom: "That must have been awfully embarrassing."

Tom: "I'm going to flunk her class—on purpose!"

Mom: "Boy, I haven't seen you this mad for a while! So what happened when you had to sing?"

Tom: "She makes me stand in the front of the room, then she plays her idiot piano. I don't even know the words! I could see Dave was giggling. I'd like to see him do it!"

Mom: "So you thought it wasn't right for her to make you do it when no one else had to."

Tom: "Yeah. Why are they picking on me all the time? What a totally ignorant school." (Tom leaves to get a snack.)

Active Listening and Self-Esteem

Active listening is a way of talking to someone with sympathy or empathy (the distinction between the two isn't important here). Active listening is very respectful of another person's thoughts and feelings, because the listener doesn't just sit there, but instead attempts (the "active" part) to see the world through the other person's eyes.

When you are listening to your child, you are—like the mother above—forgetting your own opinions for a while, suspending judgment, and committing yourself to completely understanding how the child saw a particular situation (you don't have to agree with him). In our example, Mom is not thinking that her son is being disrespectful or that he caused the trouble. Nor is she formulating her own response.

Quik Tip...
Active listening is respectful of your child's thoughts and feelings. But listening isn't easy—you have to learn to keep your own opinions to yourself for a while!

Active listening, therefore, tries to accomplish two things: (1) to understand what another person is saying and thinking—from his or her point of view, and (2) to communicate back and check your understanding with the person doing the talking. The listener is an active participant in the conversation, not someone who just sits and nods from time to time (although that's not so bad either!).

Active listening is not easy for parents. Once you get past the point of feeling artificial or too passive, you can sometimes pleasantly knock the kids right off their feet. And listening is an excellent way to begin any lengthy, serious conversation.

How Do You Do Active Listening?

First, get into the proper frame of mind: "I'm going to hear this kid out—even if it kills me—and find out exactly what he thinks." Next, you can use four different approaches. Your listening strategies include openers, nonjudgmental questions, reflecting feelings and perception checks or summaries.

Openers

You can start with what are called "openers"—brief comments or questions designed to elicit further information from your child. These comments often require self-control, and are especially difficult when you are caught off guard. Openers may also appear incredibly passive to you, but remember that active listening must precede any problem-solving discussion. If discipline or other action is necessary, worry about that after you've gotten the facts.

Openers can be very simple, such as "Oh?", "Wow!", "Yeah" or "What?" An opener can be anything that communicates that you are ready and willing to listen sympathetically, including nonverbal behavior, such as sitting down next to the youngster or putting down the paper to look at him. In the example above, Mom's opener was "Tell me what happened."

Nonjudgmental Questions

After openers, questions are often necessary to further your understanding of what a child is talking about. To be effective, these questions must not be loaded or judgmental. "Why did you do a stupid thing like that?", "What's your problem today?" or "Why are you bugging me now about this?" are not good questions. These comments will inspire argument or silence.

Here are some better questions that keep the talk going and further understanding: "What do you think made you do that?" or "What was going through your mind at the time?" In our example above, Mom asked, "So what happened when you had to sing?" That was a good question.

Reflecting Feelings

A third active listening strategy is called "reflecting feelings." If you are going to tell someone that you think you understand him, try to let him know that you can imagine how he must have *felt* under the circumstances. Sometimes, when you reflect feelings, older kids will tell you that you sound a bit like a shrink. If that's the case, just say, "Sorry, but I'm just trying to make sure I understand what you're talking about."

In the example above, Mom reflected feelings back at two points: "That must have been awfully embarrassing" and "Boy, I haven't seen you this mad for a while!" Other examples of reflecting feelings might include: "You really sound bummed out about that," "That must have really been fun!" or "You were pretty upset with me."

Reflecting feelings accomplishes several things. First, it lets the child know that whatever he is feeling is OK (it's what he may *do* about it that can be right or wrong). Second, this response reinforces self-esteem. And third, reflecting feelings also helps diffuse negative emotions so they are not acted out somewhere else. You can bet that if Tom's mother had first said, "That's no way to talk about your teachers!", his anger would have been redirected at her immediately.

Perception Checks

The name of this tactic may also sound fancy, but the idea is simple. From time to time during a talk, check out whether or not you are getting a good idea of what your youngster is saying. Perception checks tell a child that you're listening and really trying to see the world through his eyes.

Examples of perception checks or summaries might be: "Sounds like you're saying that our rules for chores favor your sister", "You felt it was your worst day at school this year" or "You wish I weren't gone so much so we could do more together?" In the example above, Mom's summary was this: "So you thought it wasn't very fair for her to make you do it when no one else had to." That was a nice, sympathetic comment.

Active listening is a communication skill, but it is also an attitude. Your attitude, not your child's. It's the attitude of sincerely trying to figure out what someone else is thinking even if you don't agree. This, of course, is a different kind of job if you're talking to a two-year-old or a ten-year-old. Either way it's a great self-esteem builder for children. You'll also learn a lot about what your children think about life. Start listening now, because you'll certainly want to stay in touch with your kids when they're teens!

> **Quik Tip...**
>
> Active listening is a skill, but it's also an attitude—on your part. Better start listening now, because you're definitely going to want to know what your kids are thinking when they're teenagers!

Active Listening and Counting

So active listening helps you to understand your children and listening also helps to diffuse negative emotions. That's fine, but if you active listened *all the time*, you wouldn't be any kind of a disciplinarian. Active listening, by itself, has nothing to do with setting limits and enforcing rules. Imagine this scene:

Son: "Mom—you idiot! My best T-shirt's still in the wash!"
Mother: "You're feeling pretty frustrated with me."

This parent's response is overly nice. It is also inappropriate. The child's disrespect is way out of proportion to the situation and should be confronted.

On the other hand, if you counted *all the time* whenever the kids were upset, you wouldn't be a very understanding parent. Your kids would correctly perceive you as only an instrument of discipline—or worse.

Imagine this summertime scenario:

"I'm bored."
"That's 1."

That's a pretty insensitive and unnecessary response. Your kids certainly won't want to talk to you very often! So how in the world is a parent supposed to know when to listen and when to count? Sometimes this decision is easy, but often it's not. Here are some guidelines.

Listen If the Kids Are Not Upset with You

If the child is upset about something that didn't have anything to do with you, it is probably time to active listen. This behavior couldn't be testing and manipulation, because you didn't do anything to frustrate the child.

Seven-year-old David, for example, runs in yelling:

> "THOSE GUYS ARE JERKS!"
> "Who's that, David?"
> "The kids across the street—they won't let me go in their yard."
> "Why not?"
> "I don't know. They're just morons."
> "Boy, you sound really upset!"
> "Yeah, I'm not playing with those creeps."
> "That sounds like a good idea."

Dad doesn't count the yelling. The problem occurred outside, not with Dad. A little active listening may diffuse the situation.

Or, back to the old summertime refrain (Amanda, 10):

> "I'm bored."
> "You're not having a very good day, huh?"
> "No. There's nothing to do."
> "You try, but you can't think of anything fun at all?"
> "Nope. Can we go get that book I wanted?"
> "I've got to go to the mall, anyway. Let's do it."
> "All right!"

Here Mom doesn't get trapped into making seven suggestions that will be shot down. Her daughter is not feeling so hot, but she isn't badgering or testing. It's time for a little sympathetic listening. If the two can work out something to do, fine. If not, see the next example.

If the Upset Switches to You

Sometimes the kids will start out upset by something else, but then their frustration will switch to the parent. In that case, try active listening, but you had better be ready to count.

Amanda's situation above is a little tricky. What if Mom doesn't want to do anything or can't go out?

"I'm bored."
"You're not having a very good day, huh?"
"No. There's nothing to do."
"You try, but you can't think of anything fun at all?"
"Nope. Can we go get that new book I wanted?"
"I can't, honey."
"Aw, why not?"
"I've got things to do here."
"What do you have to do?"
"Plenty. Look, why don't you call Megan and see if she wants to do something. I could maybe pick her up."
"If you can pick her up, why can't you take me to get my book?"
"That's 1."
"Oh for pete's sake." (Amanda leaves.)

Here Mom tries active listening, but it doesn't defuse the situation. Amanda puts the hit on her mother to be the local entertainment committee. Mom can't produce the desired services, so Amanda gets into badgering, martyrdom and intimidation. Mom catches herself getting verbally involved in the impossible, and starts counting.

Discuss Problems, Count Attacks

What if the kids are upset with you in the first place? This situation gets even trickier. It depends partly upon how the little ones approach you. In general the rule is "Discuss Problems, Count Attacks." "Mom—you idiot—my best T-shirt's still in the wash!" is an attack from the start, and many parents would give an immediate 3 for the "idiot" remark.

Some children's comments are not quite attacks, and if a parent uses a little active listening, the emotion may be diffused:

"Why are you making me do this stupid homework now!?"
"Homework's a real bummer, isn't it?"
"Oh, brother." (Child starts his homework with a sigh.)

Here the active listening helped reduce the unpleasant emotion so the child didn't act on it. Keep the 1-2-3 ready in your back pocket, though, because you may not always be so lucky:

"Why are you making me do this stupid homework now?!"
"Homework's a real bummer, isn't it?"
"Yeah, I hate it!"
"Boy, you really don't like it, do you?"
"I could be rollerblading with Jason."
"You'd really prefer to be outside playing."
"DON'T JUST SAY BACK EVERYTHING I SAY!"
"That's 1."

Remarkable presence of mind on the part of this parent.

Points to Remember...

1. You are a good active listener if, while your child is talking, you are sincerely trying to understand what he is saying.

2. You are a bad active listener if, while your child is talking, you are preparing your rebuttal.

Questions for Christian Practice

1. Read Proverbs 18:2, Proverbs 18:13 and Proverbs 18:21. How can these verses be applied to active listening?

2. When do you have trouble listening to your child?

3. Do you think your child would benefit if you became a better listener? Explain.

4. Which active listening strategy do you think will be most difficult for you? Why?

5. Active listening is a skill. When is a good time for you to practice active listening with your child (before bed, after school, at mealtimes, etc.)?

26
Your New Life

"For I know the plans I have for you," declares the Lord, "plans to prosper you and not to harm you, plans to give you hope and a future."

Jeremiah 29:11

At this point you are well into our three parenting steps. You are controlling obnoxious behavior with counting; you are using the seven Start behavior tactics to encourage good behavior (and have come up with a few of your own!); and you are consistently working on building your relationship with each of your children by means of affection, praise, listening and—most important of all—one-on-one fun.

1-2-3 Magic for Christian Parents is known for producing results. It works—and it often works in a very short period of time. No magic. It's just the logical, consistent application of biblically grounded parenting principles. Just one more caution, though, before we let you go.

Falling Off the Wagon

Nobody is perfect. Parents and teachers are human beings who have good days and bad days. Many people have used the 1-2-3 religiously for years and years. For other caretakers it is a struggle to stay consistent and to remember what you're supposed to be doing.

The problem we're talking about here is called "slipping." Some people call it backsliding. It means you start out well with *1-2-3 Magic for Christian Parents*, get the kids shaped up, but then slip back into your old unproductive ways of operating. The 1-2-3 switch sort of goes to the "Off" position. The former status quo has a nasty way of sneaking back up on us. Falling off the wagon can occur suddenly on an especially bad day, or slipping can happen more gradually over a period of months or even years.

In the course of a day it's easy to get distracted when there's always so much going on. You have to go to work, drive the kids all over the place, cook (or get fast food), answer junk phone calls, help with homework, call your mother, try to find a little time to read the paper and so on. When you're trying to do nine things at once, who can remember the No-Talking and No-Emotion Rules?

You can! It's not always easy, but it beats arguing and screaming, which only add to your troubles, making you feel angry and guilty on top of everything else. Remember: *1-2-3 Magic for Christian Parents* was specifically created for busy parents like yourself who are inevitably going to get upset from time to time.

Over the long term, slipping can occur for a number of reasons. The most frequent culprits are visitors, illness, travel, new babies and just plain time. Gradually you find yourself talking too much, getting too excited and frustrated, and not enjoying your kids anymore. Then one night, you wake up at 3:00 and wonder, "What happened to the 1-2-3?"

What do you do when you find yourself—over the short or long term—falling back into your old ways? First of all, accept slipping as normal. Nobody's perfect, including you, and you shouldn't expect yourself to be. Life—especially with kids—is also quite a bit more complex than any of us ever anticipated.

Second, it's *back to basics*. Almost invariably, when parents come to me and say "The 1-2-3 is not working anymore," what is happening is a major violation of the No-Talking and No-Emotion Rules. This point cannot be emphasized strongly enough. So we sit down and review the *1-2-3 Magic* theory and the procedures very carefully, and then send mom and dad on their way. This brief refresher course usually takes care of the problem.

Fortunately, the Stop and Start behavior methods described here are simple and can be resurrected and reapplied with little difficulty. The fact that you've used them once and slipped does not hurt their effectiveness the second time around. Turn that 1-2-3 switch back to "On."

When you have caught yourself backsliding on a bad day, you might say something like this to your kids: "Guys, I'm not doing my job right. You got me frustrated and I'm talking and yelling too much. We're going back to counting as of right now." When you've regressed over a longer period, consider redoing the Kickoff Conversation with the whole gang.

Over the course of your kids' growing-up time at your house, you may go through a number of slips and recoveries—daily, monthly or even annually. Each time you catch yourself getting careless, just pick yourself up, take a deep breath and go back to what you know works best.

A Different Future

What can you expect from *1-2-3 Magic*? You can expect a more peaceful household, a lot less arguing and fewer angry moments. You can expect more time for fun, and affection will come more easily. You will have more time and energy to devote to the Christian part of Christian parenting. The self-esteem of your children will improve. So will your self-esteem as a parent, because you will be more in control and will know you are handling things correctly. If you are a teacher, you will feel more confident, more in control of your class, and you will have more time for instruction.

What it all boils down to is this: How do you want to spend your time with your kids? One option is that you can spend your time like this:

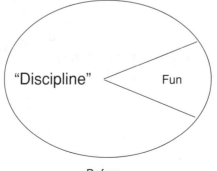

Before
1-2-3 MAGIC FOR CHRISTIAN PARENTS

Here the kids are driving you crazy most of the time. You are caught up in frequent but futile attempts at "discipline." There is little time to enjoy the children, educate them or like them.

On the other hand, you can spend your time like this:

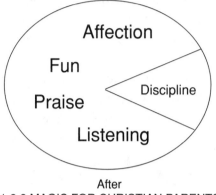

After
1-2-3 MAGIC FOR CHRISTIAN PARENTS

In this situation the proper perspective has been established. Sanity is restored by the 1-2-3, making discipline crisp, gentle and efficient. There's less arguing and yelling, and in this more peaceful atmosphere there are more good times. Everyone's self-esteem benefits.

I'll never forget one mother's comment to me years ago. When she first came into my office, her three kids were driving her nuts. We got her going on *1-2-3 Magic*, and she shaped things up at home very well. One early January day, I saw her for a followup visit. She told me Christmas vacation—with all the kids home—had actually gone quite well. She was pleasantly surprised.

Then she said something I've never forgotten: "You know what, though, I never realized how far I'd come until the kids went back to school after vacation."

"What do you mean?" I asked.

"I missed them for the first time in my life," she said.

Quite a turnaround. It's a whole new world when you get along well with—and enjoy—your own children.

Good luck!
Don't spend any more days caught up in useless irritation. Take charge of your home today—and start having some fun with your kids!

Our prayer for you is that by applying the principles of *1-2-3 Magic for Christian Parents* you will experience the benefits described in Proverbs: "Discipline your children; you'll be glad you did —they'll turn out delightful to live with" (Proverbs 29:17).

Questions for Christian Practice

1. Read Psalm 34:18, Jeremiah 23:23 and James 1:5. As a Christian parent what is the primary source you can depend on?

2. How has your family changed since implementing 1-2-3 Magic for Christian Parents?

3. What are some difficulties that could distract you from the 1-2-3 plan?

4. How will you focus more on teaching your children about Christian living now that you have more time and energy?

5. Take a moment and thank God for your children and your privilege to have them as part of your life.